ON DUTY WITH THE QUEEN

ON DUTY WITH THE QUEEN

Dickie Arbiter
with Lynne Barrett-Lee

BLINK
bringing you closer

Published by Blink Publishing
Deepdene Lodge
Deepdene Avenue
Dorking RH5 4AT, UK

www.blinkpublishing.co.uk

facebook.com/blinkpublishing
twitter.com/blinkpublishing

978-1-905825-86-8

A CIP catalogue of this book is available from the British Library.

Typeset by Fakenham Prepress Solutions

Printed and bound by Clays Ltd, St Ives Plc

3 5 7 9 10 8 6 4

© Dickie Arbiter with Lynne Barrett-Lee, 2014
All images courtesy of Getty, except images one and two (courtesy of Dickie
Arbiter); image five (Rex Features); image eight (Rex Features); image eleven
(image2photo.co.uk) and image twelve (Rex Features).

Papers used by Blink Publishing are natural, recyclable products made from
wood grown in sustainable forests. The manufacturing processes conform to
the environmental regulations of the country of origin.

Every reasonable effort has been made to trace copyright holders of material
reproduced in this book, but if any have been inadvertently overlooked the
publishers would be glad to hear from them.

Blink Publishing is an imprint of the Bonnier Publishing Group
www.bonnierpublishing.co.uk

For Victoria, who never once complained

Acknowledgments

For years I steadfastly refused to put pen to paper until my agent Sylvia Tidy-Harris persuaded me otherwise. She convinced me that my life has been one big story and that my time at Buckingham Palace was just one chapter in it, so my thanks to Sylvia for having faith.

Thank you to my literary agent, Andrew Lownie, for seeing the big picture and to Lynne Barrett-Lee for transposing my chat into something readable.

I would also like to thank Blink Publishing and my editor Joel Simons, who sometimes must have been tearing his hair out.

A big thank you to my daughter Victoria and son-in-law Ryan Brown, who between them brushed off all the cobwebs and reminded me of some of life's episodes I didn't think important.

Finally to Rosemary, my wife of thirty years, without whom none of this would have been possible.

Contents

CONTENTS

Prologue

August 1997

A car approached as I walked up the private road towards Kensington Palace.

The driver-side window wound down as the vehicle slowed, and I realised it was Diana. She smiled and waved as she always did before moving on her way. She looked happy. I knew she would be heading back to the South of France imminently. She had just been on holiday there with her boys, but now that they were in Scotland with the rest of the Royal Family, she was planning to return at the invitation of her friend, Dodi Fayed. They were in the midst of a brief summer romance, a simple flirtation at best, but I was glad to know she wouldn't be by herself for the remainder of the school holidays.

The memory of that neighbourly exchange between the Princess and me some two weeks prior played in my head as I sat, transfixed by the live news images of a car lying twisted and mangled in the depths of a tunnel in Paris.

Details were scarce, but at least she was alive. Paul Burrell, Diana's butler, kept running into our apartment, sobbing, desperate for an update. I had checked in with the office, but as yet they didn't know anything more than what I was seeing on television.

I turned, startled by the ringing phone. It was just after 3am. It was Penny Russell-Smith, the Buckingham Palace duty press secretary.

'She's gone…' was all she said.

I showered, dressed and left for the office.

CHAPTER I

Into *Britannia*

May 1988 – Sydney, Australia

'If you were approached to join the Palace press office to look after the Prince and Princess of Wales, would you be interested?'

It was Friday 15th April – the eve of my departure for Australia, where I would be covering the Queen's bicentennial tour for IRN (Independent Radio News) that I received the phone call from Philip Mackie, one of the Queen's press secretaries, which would radically change my life.

Perhaps it was his distinctive Scottish brogue, difficult to decipher at the best of times. Or maybe what I'd heard him say couldn't be what he'd actually said. I asked him to repeat the question, and much to my astonishment I had heard him correctly.

To say I was shocked would be putting it mildly, and the conversation took a long time to sink in. But as I finished packing for the tour, I was struck by a profound sense of anticipation. Switching camps, turning from poacher to gamekeeper, seemed like the natural next step in my career.

I was almost 48, and in the market for a change of plan. I was working for LBC News Radio (London Broadcasting Company) which, together with IRN, had a retirement age set at 60. With the date ever looming, I had begun to wonder if I should do something else with the next dozen years of my working life. Should I remain at LBC, doing much the same as I already was? Should I take my talents elsewhere? Do similar work for another broadcaster? Or should I change direction altogether? I didn't know. I just had the feeling that I ought to be doing *something*.

This is not to say I didn't enjoy my current job. I was one of two accredited Court Correspondents to Buckingham Palace, the other being the Press Association's Tom Corby. As neither the BBC nor ITN had such roles (Sky News didn't begin to broadcast until 1989), we were the only two Court Correspondents in the UK. It gave me an extraordinary degree of autonomy and privilege, as there was no steadfast criterion to my everyday role that wasn't self-implemented. If I wasn't on the beat covering a royal story, there was always a daily visit to the Buckingham Palace press office to clear my in-tray of announcements, investiture lists, and the 'Wednesday List' of royal engagements, which also provided an opportunity to chat with whichever press secretaries happened to be in the office at the time.

I also travelled a great deal. As a reporter covering the many varied royal engagements, it came with the territory, though not always to the extent that I would have preferred. That particular year had begun with another visit to Australia, this one undertaken by the Prince and Princess of Wales to celebrate the country's 200th anniversary. Knowing just how popular the royal double act was, especially then – with speculation rife about the state of their marriage – I had tried hard to persuade IRN to send me with them. Citing budget issues, the answer was an emphatic no. The plan instead was to use coverage from various news agencies. As the royal couple toured, and as I had predicted, British television stations were awash with coverage, and IRN's decision was proving to be the wrong one.

The company's obligation to the network was to do exactly what it had failed to do – provide coverage of a major news story. So when I broached the subject of going on the Queen's own bicentennial tour in April and May, I got an immediate thumbs-up. I'm sure the decision had more than a little to do with the fact that between the two tours LBC/IRN had been taken over…by an Australian media group.

The flight time from London Heathrow to Perth was 18 hours. While I'd normally use the time to read or catch up on sleep, I couldn't seem to settle well to either. I don't believe there was a moment during the entire flight when I didn't think about the previous night's conversation. And yet, I couldn't discuss it. I was sworn to secrecy, so I did the only thing I could – pushed it to the back of my mind and concentrated on the job at hand.

Today, around-the-clock news is the norm, but back in the 1980s, it was still quite unusual. Even then IRN was a 24-hour news service with a voracious appetite for material. The job was made all the more challenging given that we were working long before the days of the internet, and were only on the cusp of the mobile phone revolution.

We touched down in Perth on Saturday, 16th April. It was my first visit to Australia, and I was looking forward to the upcoming tour itinerary. Perth was beautiful, with golden beaches and a way of life that put me in mind of my days spent in Rhodesia (now Zimbabwe) as a young man. That said, it was somewhat parochial back in those days. They still had liquor laws that forbade drinking on Sundays unless one was a guest at a hotel.

Happily for us journalists, with three days to spare *at the hotel* before the royal couple arrived, we were able to play as well as work. First impressions always count, and mine were overwhelmingly positive. I found the Australians friendly and very hospitable to us 'Poms'. I also took the opportunity to look up some old friends from Rhodesia, who had emigrated to the city back in the early 1980s.

Within ten days, the formal approach regarding the job offer to which Philip Mackie had alluded finally came through, during an official reception aboard the Royal Yacht *Britannia*. It was coming to the end of the Australian summer, but I was still feeling the heat. I was dressed in full black-tie regalia, ready for the reception that Her Majesty the Queen and the Duke of Edinburgh were hosting that evening, giving them a chance to mingle with Sydney's great and good. There was only one unwritten rule with which everyone complied, that nothing said by the royal couple would be quoted, repeated or reported.

It would be my first time in the yacht, which was an honour in itself, but as I hurried down to meet the mini-bus that would pick me up from my hotel, I was much more preoccupied with the thought of another honour that might just be coming my way.

As the bus approached the port, I could see the yacht tied up to the quay, the Sydney Harbour Bridge forming a majestic backdrop. No picture could ever do it justice. The yacht was small, but no less magnificent. Floodlit, she was dressed with bunting, the flag of the Lord High Admiral (the Queen) on the foremast, the Royal Standard on mainmast and the Union flag on the mizzenmast. One doesn't go *on* board the Royal Yacht *Britannia*, one goes *in* it. Sounds counter-intuitive, but as I had learned two years previously while covering a royal visit to China, Royal Yacht *Britannia* was one of the Queen's official residences, which meant that it was treated as a palace, rather than as a ship. She was a spectacular presence, steeped in a rich personal history.

The Queen relished her time in *Britannia*. Though the ship was being used in an official capacity for the tour, countless family holidays had also been spent aboard over the years. The yacht provided a sanctuary, a place where the family could spend quality time together without the burden of being on parade. At the start of many a summer break, the Windsors would cruise the Western Isles of

Scotland, mooring to picnic on remote beaches, free from prying eyes. As children in 1954, Prince Charles and his sister, Princess Anne, sailed in *Britannia* on her maiden voyage to Grand Harbour, Malta, where they were to meet their parents following the Queen and Prince Philip's six-month tour of the Commonwealth. Charles and his bride would later honeymoon aboard in 1981. She was first and foremost a family home, which is no doubt why the Queen was seen to shed a tear when the ship was decommissioned in 1997. With 44 years of happy memories, it was as though she was losing a lifelong friend.

Britannia was to be the royals' home for the rest of the tour, and she had sailed to meet the Queen and Duke of Edinburgh upon their arrival in Sydney. Now I was one of the lucky members of the press to be invited aboard. I pinched myself as I reached the top of the gangway. I was boarding one of the world's most famous yachts in one of the world's most iconic harbours to discuss a job working for the British Royal Family. I hoped my dad was up there somewhere, looking down. Having fled Berlin in the early 1930s to escape the Nazis before the outbreak of the Second World War, I always felt his presence, and I knew that he would be immensely proud.

Robin Janvrin, the press secretary, approached me with something of a twinkle in his eye. I liked Robin. He looked much younger than his 42 years, had a boyish smile and a dry sense of humor. He was ex-Royal Navy and ex-Foreign Office, so fitted the royal household mould perfectly... which, on paper, I certainly did not.

He pulled me into what I would eventually come to know as the press secretary's cabin for a meeting along with Private Secretary Sir William Heseltine. I had known Bill for a number of years, though I had only known Robin for 18 months, as he had joined the press office in the autumn of 1987.

Bill asked if I was interested in taking over from Philip Mackie upon his retirement, and whether I had any questions. I had none.

'Yes, I'm interested.'

'Great,' he replied. 'Get in touch with Robin once you're back in London and he will talk you through the nuts and bolts.'

That was it. It appeared the job was mine. We hadn't discussed terms. In fact, we hadn't discussed anything, but that didn't matter to me one jot. An offer like that only comes along once in a lifetime. It was validation of my professionalism as a journalist to have been asked. Needless to say, the remainder of that particular reception was a blur.

The three-week tour took in a large chunk of the country. We visited Perth, Geraldton, and Kalgoorlie in Western Australia, and Hobart and Launceston in Tasmania. We then traveled to Geelong in Victoria (where Prince Charles went to school in 1965) before moving on to Longreach in Queensland, where Qantas, Australia's national airline, as well as the country's flying doctor service were born. While we were there, the Queen opened the Stockman's Hall of Fame and Outback Heritage Centre. Next it was on to Brisbane to open Expo '88 before wrapping up in Sydney, Newcastle and Albury in New South Wales, and the ACT (Australian Capital Territory) Canberra, where she was to open the New Parliament House.

Royal tours are organized down to the minutest detail. It is the press secretaries' job to organize hotels, ground transportation and internal flights for the media, while also coordinating with the federal government's Department of Information. Tours are well-oiled machines, but this was the first time I had paid particular attention to the complex role I was soon to inherit.

On the flight back to London, I thought hard about the potential task ahead. Having special responsibility for the Prince and Princess of Wales was a daunting prospect. The rumour mill about the state of the Wales' marriage wasn't quite yet in overdrive, but it was increasingly being talked and written about. If my instincts were correct, the story would only get bigger. I'd be taking on the job at a volatile time. The situation could go one of two ways – things would either work out for the couple or they wouldn't.

Regardless, Charles and Diana were under intense scrutiny by the media, and as their press secretary, I would have to be on my toes. Was I up to the challenge of being on the other side of the fence with a gossip-hungry media pack at my door? Could I be up front when it was required and stonewall when necessary? Could I steer a course through what would doubtless be a stormy public relations period? I had been an outsider looking in, so I knew what to expect. It would be challenging, but I was sure I could do it. As the plane landed, I was buzzing with anticipation, but I still couldn't share my exciting news with anyone, not even my wife and daughter.

There was one person, however, whom I did need to take into my confidence – my boss, Bill Coppen-Gardner, LBC's Managing Director. I had to tell him that I was resigning, but I wasn't worried. We spent time together socially, and I knew that whatever I said to him in confidence would remain with him alone.

Despite my excitement, telling Bill of my decision would still make for a sad day, marking the end of a personal era.

LBC had been the first commercial radio station to go on-air in the UK in October 1973. I had been put in touch with the station through the well-known journalist, Ron Onions, who had begun his career working with the BBC before moving on to run the newsroom at fledgling music station Capital Radio. He informed me that LBC was actively seeking broadcasters, having launched the network solely with newspaper journalists. While the scribes were excellent writers, they were not particularly good at speaking into a microphone. I joined the station in June 1974, and not long after, Ron was brought in to serve as the Head of LBC. Ron pioneered a new style of radio programming, and it was thanks to his vision and drive that LBC went from strength to strength, knocking the BBC off its perch as it went. Along with guiding my career, Ron made household names of Bob Holness and Douglas Cameron, while also launching the careers of Jon Snow and Peter Allen. It was Ron who first assigned me the royal beat, and ensured that I was accredited by the Palace as IRN's Court Correspondent. Flattered to have been given a specialist reporting job, I asked him one day, 'Why me?'

'You speak well, with a distinctive broadcasting voice. You're always dressed properly in a suit, and by all appearances I could take you anywhere, including Buckingham Palace.'

On that basis, the job was mine.

The royal beat aside, LBC afforded me many a novel experience. In 1986 I climbed the stairs to the top of Nelson's Column in Trafalgar Square to interview the man responsible for cleaning the great Admiral himself. The uninterrupted view across London from 169.3 feet high was spectacular. Though I do not suffer from vertigo, my courage was put to the test yet again when I was asked to abseil from the ceiling of Earl's Court Exhibition Centre during the *AM* breakfast show. As I dropped 50 feet into the Royal Tournament arena, I promoted the live broadcast that I would be conducting that night. I covered Derby Day at Epsom, Royal Ascot and every ceremonial event on the royal calendar. To say LBC was a fun place to work would be doing the station a disservice. I was there at a special time, when many a long-standing career was launched. It was consistently at the forefront of breaking news. I had seen it grow, followed its fortunes and watched it beat the BBC's *Today* program on Radio 4 for a majority share of the London audience. But, alas, in recent years I had also seen its authority as a news station diminish.

Saying goodbye to it was ultimately the right thing to do. I had always been something of a challenge seeker. I knew I was about to take my place on a stage rife with thrills and spills, but when on 30th June, 1988 I walked out of LBC's Gough Square Studios for the last time, it was with only the briefest backward glance. The following day, I crossed the forecourt of Buckingham Palace with a renewed vitality, and bounded up the front steps to the Privy Purse Door.

This was it.

My next job.

My next rollercoaster ride…and what a ride it would turn out to be.

CHAPTER 2

Hanging Up the Microphone
July 1988 – London

I felt very comfortable entering Buckingham Palace that first morning. It was a place to which I had been going on a regular basis for a number of years, and as such had enjoyed virtually unchallenged access. I already knew my way around pretty well.

Yes, I was based in the same place and going to work with the same people – people with whom I had an established relationship – but now I had a completely different role. I was firmly on the inside looking out towards my former colleagues, and more importantly, I was one of the team whose job it was to manage how the Royal Family was presented.

I was welcomed by everyone in the press office, and at 10am Robin Janvrin held his daily morning meeting. The forthcoming State Visit to London by President Turgut Özal of Turkey was top of the agenda. I was well versed regarding State Visits because I had covered a great many of them, but from this day on, I would be working alongside the planning team.

Following the morning meeting I was taken on a tour of the offices. It was a way of putting a stamp on my arrival, emphasizing that I was no longer a hack but a member of the royal household. Mid-morning, Philip Mackie, the incumbent I was succeeding, walked me across Green Park to St James's Palace to meet the Prince and Princess of Wales's team. A large group of tourists lined the Palace railings in the hope of spotting a member of the Royal Family. Being the subject of the crowd's excited scrutiny was a novel experience, and an insight into what it must feel like to exist within the goldfish bowl of global celebrity.

In the coming weeks and months, I'd make the run to St James's Palace often, up to three or four times a day was the norm. If a royal story broke, or more dramatically, was *about* to break, it really was a 'run'. Fleet Street snappers would descend upon the gates and it was my job to control them.

For a reporter there's a *lot* of running around. Running to cover a story, running to get to the next story, and then negotiating the complexities of London's transport system to get back to the studio to edit the tape. That was the way I had always kept fit, but life had changed. Despite the dashes to St James's, I was now primarily based at the Palace. Given the long days I knew I'd invariably be working, it was time to establish a new exercise regime.

I was never much of a jogger, but I did enjoy

swimming, and I knew there was a pool in the Palace, tucked just behind the Belgian Suite. I decided that one of the first things I'd do was enquire about the guidelines for household staff using it. I went to see the Master of the Household, Rear Admiral Sir Paul Greening. Paul was very much a people person, having been a career officer in the Royal Navy and, prior to joining the Royal Household at Buckingham Palace, commander of the Royal Yacht *Britannia*. He had also been responsible for planning the Prince and Princess of Wales's honeymoon in 1981.

'Yes, you can indeed use the pool,' he confirmed when I asked him. 'Just as long as it's not at a time when a member of the Royal Family is using it.'

This mostly referred Diana, an avid swimmer who took to the pool most days at 7am. Princess Margaret liked to take her dip late morning, 'which is probably why it's a bit overheated,' Paul added dryly.

He also told me I could leave my towel and trunks there. 'As long as you don't leave them lying around,' he added, with his characteristic military attention to detail.

So that was me sorted. I'd always been an early riser. Living in Windsor and working in central London, it was something of a necessity, given the traffic. I would simply start early enough to cram in my swim and be out of the pool before Diana arrived. I began a daily morning swim the following Monday – a ritual I would continue for the next three or four years, till the time when the increased chlorination – insisted upon by Princess Margaret – began affecting my eyes.

In the meantime, it turned out to be the perfect routine. As on-the-job perks go, it seemed a pretty cool one, no matter how overheated the water.

I had already met the two royals whom I would ultimately answer to. As a reporter I'd interviewed the Prince of Wales regarding various environmental issues over the years, and had always admired him. Meeting him and his bride-to-be in 1981, just two days shy of their wedding, had been particularly special. I was the lead commentator for IRN's coverage of the royal wedding alongside Brian Hayes, and I was privileged to have been granted 40 minutes with the couple in the Chinese Dining Room at Buckingham Palace.

The Chinese Dining Room gets its name from its furniture, which was bought by the Prince Regent, later to become King George IV. It had originally been bought for the Brighton Pavilion – the extravagant folly the Prince had created as a royal retreat. Queen Victoria didn't have a lot of time for the place, so, during her reign, she sold it to the Brighton Corporation and had the furniture put into storage. It wasn't until early in the reign of King George V that it was moved into Buckingham Palace to grace the room it still sits in today.

Little did I know when I travelled to the Palace to chat to the Prince and his young fiancée that evening that not only would I go on to attend numerous meetings in that same room, but 16 years after the wedding itself, I would be part of the team sitting around the same table, planning the late Diana, Princess of Wales's funeral.

On that day, however, all was positive and expectant; it

was a landmark meeting. It was also unusual, in that the then press secretary, Michael Shea, had given no guidance as to what could or could not be asked. Nothing was off limits. Due to Prince Charles's unguarded comment about 'whatever in love means,' when the couple had been interviewed upon the announcement of their engagement, I couldn't help but wonder if more intriguing snippets were to come.

As it happened, nothing revealing came from the meeting, but over a cup of tea it was possible to at least gauge the feelings of the rather naïve, attractive 20-year-old girl who was going to be the focus of an unprecedented amount of global attention. It was also a first glimpse into the character of the woman who I would later come to call boss. Diana told me that her wedding day would be an overwhelming experience, but that she was not so much concerned for herself as she was for her father – the 8th Earl Spencer. In 1978 he'd suffered a stroke that had left him quite unsteady. She explained that he was still determined to do his fatherly duty and walk his youngest daughter down the aisle of St Paul's Cathedral – an aisle that was a daunting 210 feet long.

I remember being touched by her capacity for caring and understanding. Putting other people's needs before her own was a trait for which she would very soon come to be known, and one which I would witness time and again.

I had been broadcasting for 15 years at the time of Charles and Diana's wedding on Wednesday, 29th July, 1981. In the months leading up to the big day I was charged with organizing all of the outside broadcast commentary points along the processional route from Buckingham Palace to St Paul's Cathedral – eight sites in all. I had decided that I would spend the day in the commentary booth on the Queen Victoria Memorial outside Buckingham Palace. I could have chosen any one of the eight sites, but I wanted to be right at the heart of the occasion, witnessing both the beginning and the end of the day's celebrations.

My morning started with a sound check in the commentary booth at 5am, to ensure that everything was in working order. At 6am I was on the air setting the scene for listeners tuned into the *AM* breakfast show, and I continued to feed into other programming as the day progressed. Our coverage for IRN went out across the whole of the commercial radio network dotted throughout the UK – England, Ireland, Scotland and Wales. Royal events are organised down to the very last minute, which allowed for us to tailor our coverage accordingly. The day had been given over entirely to coverage of all things relating to the royal wedding.

The Queen's carriage procession left the Palace at 10:22am. The procession, eight carriages long, conveyed every member of the Royal Family, 21 in total, to St Paul's Cathedral. The groom's procession – Prince Charles, accompanied by his brother, Prince Andrew, who was to act as his supporter – left at 10:30am.

A wedding is always a happy occasion, but this had been the most anticipated royal wedding in recent history. Some one million spectators lined the processional route to take in the sense of occasion, the pomp and pageantry. The joyful atmosphere across London was arresting. And it wasn't just limited to the Union flag-clad masses. The Queen, often perceived as rather dour, beamed throughout the day's proceedings. From the moment she left Buckingham Palace in the morning, to when she ran across the Palace forecourt to wave goodbye to Charles and Diana as they left for their honeymoon at 4pm, the Queen was in her element.

Much has been written about the presence of Mrs Camilla Parker Bowles in the congregation at St Paul's that day. Simply put, there was no reason why she should not have been there and every reason why she should have been. There was no animosity between Diana and Camilla. She was a long-standing friend of Prince Charles. Her husband, Andrew Parker Bowles, played polo with the Prince regularly, and on the wedding day, Lieutenant Colonel Andrew Parker Bowles was commanding the Sovereign's Escort of the Household Cavalry, which led the Queen's carriage procession.

Did Charles and Diana love each other? Yes they did, and it was readily apparent in those early days. I witnessed many an occasion when Charles couldn't keep his hands off her. He would often rest his hand on her forearm, and every now and then give her bottom a light pat when they were out and about on engagements. To suggest that they were never in love is pure conjecture.

Reflecting on that July day, everything looked to be so promising in terms of a long and happy marriage for Charles and Diana. The Queen and the Duke of Edinburgh had been married almost 34 years, and everyone hoped for an equally harmonious union for the next generation.

More than once, Diana told me that she never wanted a divorce. She had, after all, been a child of divorce herself. Unfortunately, their marriage was at the mercy of an insatiable media from day one. No doubt this contributed to its very public 'he said/she said' deterioration which sadly forced them to call an end to their marriage once and for all.

I suppose the only strange thing about my first day as a press secretary was picking up the office phone to answer my first press call. Suddenly I was responding to the questions instead of asking them. It was an odd feeling, but as I settled into my new role I began to realise that this was a job that was going to suit me perfectly.

Once I'd had my swim, my first task every day was to scour the daily newspapers for stories; not only royal stories but those which included any mention of the word 'royal'. I would mark up the pieces so that a synopsis could be delivered to the Queen. Then it was off to press office meetings, Prince of Wales office meetings and the business of strategizing upcoming royal engagements. I took to the job like a duck to water, but continued to find it remarkable that I had even landed the position in the first place. After all, the Royal Family didn't employ people like me. I didn't have any qualifications to speak of. I had no university education. I hadn't served in the British military, and I had no experience working in government. I was for all intents and purposes a hack. All I knew was that I had come a long way from where I had begun.

*

I was born in north west London, in September 1940, about four-and-a-half miles from the royal Palace in which I now worked. I was the son of German Jews. My father, Hans, had left Berlin in 1930 to escape Nazi persecution, and my mother Ruth had left Aachen in 1939 to do the same. My own arrival had occurred in rather inauspicious circumstances. Thanks to the kindness of my mother's cousin I came into the world in a private clinic in Finchley Road. I was born in the middle of an air raid courtesy of the *Luftwaffe*, though I imagine the bombing was the last thing on my mother's mind. I doubt there are many things all-consuming enough to distract one from the fact that she might be blasted out of existence at any moment, but I suspect being in the throes of labour was probably one of them.

It was to be a long time, however, before I would have any sort of meaningful dialogue with the young woman who gave birth to me. She left my father and in turn me when I was just four years old. I never did discover the precise reason why. It might have had something to do with the fact that she was a vibrant 23-year old who had married a man who was not only in his 40s, but also desperately stricken with TB and diabetes.

Ill as my father was, I imagine my mother's leaving must have been devastating for him. She was his second wife – he'd divorced the first back in Berlin, and meeting someone as young and lively as my mother must have felt like a miraculous second chance. They met during a card game at the home of my mother's cousin, Alphons, in London. She had arrived in the city aged 17, and he'd provided board and lodging for her, though not for nothing. He was in publishing and haute couture and was quite well off, but in exchange for a roof over her head my mother had to sing for her supper – cleaning both his apartment and his West End showroom.

He also had her help him when he was entertaining. One of the social preoccupations amongst the German Jewish refugee community in London at that time was to play cards – usually poker. My father was a regular player at cousin Alphons's table, and as my mother frequently attended the card games, serving food and drinks, it wasn't long before romance began to blossom. Within six months of her arrival in England, they were married.

Though the sudden disappearance of my mother must have been a great blow to my father, it wasn't as traumatic for me. With the constant air raids and bombing, our lives were already punctuated by regular episodes of violent drama, so perhaps her leaving simply blended in to the daily angst we were already experiencing. My only memory of her during that early part of my life wasn't even a particularly fond one. She was a stickler for table manners, and to ensure that mealtimes were conducted with a degree of decorum, she would make me sit at the table with a London telephone directory under each arm, to ensure I didn't eat with my elbows sticking out like chicken wings.

Did she think that I might one day find myself eating with the aristocracy? I doubt it. All I knew was that a volume of the London telephone directory in the

1940s – of which there were four, each about two inches thick: A-D, E-K, L-R, S-Z – was a pretty heavy thing to have clamped under one's armpits, whichever part of the alphabet was involved.

Unhappy as my father no doubt was, my mother's departure brought a period of relative calm. And with no more phone directories at the table, one of happiness as well. My father was a kind and gentle man and I adored him. I was quite happy with it being just the two of us, but sadly, this wasn't to last. Had he been able, I don't doubt he would have brought me up singlehandedly, but he also had to make a living to support us both. So while he went to work at the family belt manufacturing business, he left me in the 'care' of a German au pair.

My new nemesis was much more trying than a pair of phone books. She was called Eva, and looking back, I think she must have learned her craft as a concentration camp guard. I had no evidence of this, but there seemed no other explanation for her apparently random, but regular acts of cruelty. If I made her cross, she would squeeze my hand so tightly that it would go scarlet, and for more serious misdemeanors, her punishment of choice was a swift Chinese burn to the wrist. If I had to get up in the night to go to the lavatory, she would follow me, switching off all the lights as quickly as I had switched them on, making terrifying ghostly noises as she went. Eva was evil.

Still, it was a largely harmonious time, as I was surrounded by my father's family. We all lived in the same block in West Hampstead – Embassy House, which remains standing to this day. We were at number 44; dad's brother Fritz and his wife, another Ruth, and their 11-year old son, Peter, were at number 35. Lastly, at number 2, lived my dad's other (single) brother, Eric. My father's housekeeper, Mrs Eldridge, lived just up the road from us, and she was a friendly, very maternal presence in my life.

Unusually for the time, the Eldridges owned their own house, and Bill Eldridge, who was a builder, had converted their coal cellar into a comfortable air raid shelter. When the sirens went off, we'd all troop down into the womb-like interior, where, with the raids invariably continuing overnight, I'd fall into a deep and peaceful sleep.

Coming up following the all-clear was invigorating, as, with the benefit of childlike optimism, I always greeted whatever sight I found with excitement rather than fear...even on the day I returned to find my bed buried under rubble from a bedroom wall that was no longer standing.

It was a halcyon period that was to be cut very short. I was aware that my father was ill, and that sometimes he had to go to hospital, so when he disappeared off to a sanatorium in Switzerland, shortly after my sixth birthday, I don't remember thinking anything of it. I would usually be billeted with Uncle Fritz and Aunt Ruth during these times, and I'd become quite used to being shuttled back and forth. But on New Year's Eve 1946 it seemed there would no longer be a 'back'. My uncle broke the news to me that my beloved father had passed away.

I had no grandparents to speak of. On my father's side, I vaguely remember being taken into a bedroom when I was three or four years old to visit an old man lying in bed with his eyes closed and his mouth hanging open. To this day I haven't a clue as to whether or not he was alive, but I was told to kiss him before being ushered back out of the room. I didn't see him again.

There was never any mention of my paternal grandmother.

I didn't fare much better on my mother's side. Her mother, Else, had walked out on her father when she was just 13-years-old. Else had met another man who had seen the writing on the wall in Nazi Germany and secured exit permits for both of them. With no hesitation they married and left Germany to begin a new life together in Argentina. My mother never saw her again.

My mother's father, Josef, managed to secure exit permits for my mother and her brother Harry. He escorted them both to London to ensure that they were safely settled in the city before returning to Germany to wind up his business. To escape being arrested, he slept at the home of various non-Jewish friends before he was betrayed, captured and put on a train bound for a concen-tration camp. He never made it. Knowing all too well what lay in store he was forced to make an unimaginable choice. As the train traveled at full speed, he climbed out of the carriage and jumped onto the rails below, killing himself. My mother and her brother were all that was left of the family she once knew.

I recall little of either the day or the conversation that

ensued when the news came that my father had died, but other discussions were now underway, chiefly about what the family was going to do with me. With my mother gone from my life, I was technically an orphan, and though I had two uncles, it seemed neither was in a position to look after me. Uncle Fritz was fit and well, but barely had space in his flat to house his own little family, and my other uncle, Eric, was no more of a well man than my father had been as he suffered from what we today know as motor neurone disease. The nature of his illness meant that his health was only going to deteriorate, and it was decided that, in the short term at least, the best thing would be to pack me off to a boarding school.

I was dispatched to the newly established Holme Grange Preparatory School in Wokingham just days after the news that my father wasn't coming home. It was early January 1947, one of the coldest winters on record. The weather was in tune with the way I was feeling. I was not quite six-and-a-half years old, and it's difficult to describe just how desolate I felt. My Uncle Eric was charged with taking me to school, and I remember standing with him at Waterloo station, feeling a powerful urge to just abandon my newly acquired trunk and run away, but an hour and a half later, my fate was sealed.

The school was a converted Grade II listed former manor house – a large red brick pile built in 1883 by the architect Norman Shaw. It had an imposing and very grand wooden front door, the like of which I had never seen before. We arrived from the station by taxi, and were met on the steps by Mr Gordon-Walker.

After a cold and rather perfunctory greeting I was simply passed into the hands of a senior boy called Asher. Uncle Eric was dismissed with an obligatory farewell by my new headmaster, and that was that. The deed was done. My welcome to the school was over in the space of ten minutes, and I burst into floods of tears.

It was grim. The snow began falling not long after I arrived there, but there was no childish excitement in my heart. It was bitterly cold and there was no heating – a situation made all the worse by post-war food and fuel shortages. The headmaster was a stickler for fresh air, so fresh air we got. The freezing dormitories were even chillier due to the constant arctic blast, which made the starched sheets we slept between feel like icy slabs. I cried my eyes out the first night and for many nights afterwards. I just couldn't stop, which was perhaps apt, because it became readily apparent that there would be much more to cry about over the coming weeks and months.

Should anyone be sent to boarding school at six? Not in my opinion. But it wasn't just my age that made the experience so horrible. Like many schools of its kind, the regime, which was probably billed as 'character-building' at the time, was brutal in its cruelty. Along with most new boys, I was bullied mercilessly, not least because at this stage I spoke English with a clipped German accent. Given the recent global events this inevitably made me a target. I was also fairly scrawny. Many of the youngest and smallest boys were bullied, which was only to be expected in an institution run by a hard-drinking headmaster who presided over a school with physical punishment woven into its very fabric. I was soon to learn one didn't need to do anything terribly wrong to feel the sting of a cane. Indeed, he told me within a day of my tearful arrival that all the boys' parents and guardians had given him permission to use the cane whenever he felt like it. Looking back I doubt that was true, but he certainly seemed to feel like it a lot.

I coped with it, only just, but there was a glimmer of hope as I approached my seventh birthday. News came that I had never expected to hear. I was finally to be reunited with my mother.

CHAPTER 3

Outward Bound

August 1988

I had been in my new job for just under a month when another equally unexpected piece of news came my way. Just as 40 years previously I had been summoned to meet my mother, so I was now being called upon to meet the Queen at her Scottish retreat, Balmoral Castle.

Her Majesty departs for her favourite home in late July every year and returns to London mid-October. I was surprised that she had extended the invitation for me to join her there.

As head of state, she was ultimately my boss, but as my duties didn't relate to her specifically it had never occurred to me that I might be invited for any sort of audience.

I'd met the Queen before. During the course of my work as a royal correspondent, I had encountered her at press receptions on three previous occasions in Jordan, China and Australia, so she certainly knew who I was. But this was something very different indeed.

'You'll fly up there,' Robin Janvrin informed me, 'and you'll be picked up by a suite car. Make sure you pack for all eventualities.'

I didn't know exactly how to prepare, but three weeks later I caught a flight from Heathrow to Aberdeen, carrying everything I thought I might conceivably need: my dinner jacket – formal dining was always a black-tie affair for the Royal Family – some casual clothes, some appropriate footwear and my trusty Barbour jacket, leaving my jeans, trainers and T-shirts at home.

It was just as well I brought the Barbour. As we descended into Aberdeen, the low charcoal skies performed entirely to expectation, dumping biblical quantities of rain.

I didn't care. This was already quite an adventure. Not only had I never been to Balmoral, I had never been to Scotland. For all my globetrotting, I'd not so much as placed a foot on Scottish soil, so as the driver took me on the 75-minute journey from Aberdeen's Dyce Airport to Balmoral Castle, I had nothing but vague stereotypes to inform me of what to expect – terrible weather, incredible scenery, distilleries, bagpipes and kilts.

As for the Scottish way of life, I was largely in the dark. I knew the daily routine at Balmoral was outdoorsy and informal, but even that didn't prepare me for what the footman, whose job it was to greet and brief me, told me upon arrival.

'If you'd like to get changed, Sir,' – Household guests are always addressed as 'sir' or 'ma'am' (rhyming with jam) – 'and make your way back down within half an hour. I believe you're going on a picnic.'

The footman read the incredulous look on my face. If a picnic in the pouring rain was a surprise, it was nothing compared to the one that would greet me half an hour later. As I waited in the entrance hall, now duly clothed for the occasion, I became aware of a 5ft 4inch whirlwind who seemed to have appeared out of nowhere. She flashed past me, carried on through the open front door and barked 'come along, then, get in!'

Though I was stunned by the vision I was even more disorientated by the realization that what came naturally – going around to open the waiting Land Rover's door for her – wasn't required here. Indeed, by the time I had obeyed orders and opened the passenger door, she was already in the car, behind the wheel, with the engine running. We set off at quite a lick, arriving at the picnic spot, a small wooden lodge, about 15 minutes later. I was similarly instructed to get out.

The whole scene was surreal. I can't remember a single thing we had to eat. What I do remember was the incredible informality of it all. Our group included the Queen and me, Prince Philip – to whom I remember chatting about Rhodesia, wildlife and conservation – and Mary Morrison, a lady-in-waiting. The Queen served lunch out of Tupperware, not fine china, and the conversation flowed as readily as the rain.

It was wonderful, free of pomp and ceremony, and it felt like the most natural thing in the world to start clearing the table at the end of the meal.

The Queen joined me in the kitchen inside the wooden lodge. I had already run water and added a squirt of washing-up liquid. With my hands immersed in the suds, I quipped, 'I'll wash, you dry.'

'No,' she said in a quiet but firm voice. 'I'll wash, *you* dry.'

Picking up a tea towel, I dried my hands and duly did as I was told. It was an extraordinary start to an unforgettable 24 hours.

After the picnic it was back to the 'big house' to change clothes and head out for a walk. The Queen, a country woman at heart and at her happiest at Balmoral, set a cracking pace. We spent more than an hour traversing a two-mile stretch alongside Loch Muik, the corgis at our feet. She would stop every so often to clear the leaves or stones that blocked the flow of water from some of the many streams that ran into the Loch. We passed *Glas-Allt Shiel*, a large cottage built as a holiday home by Queen Victoria in 1860. She used it often during widowhood, and the Queen told me it was still occasionally used by her family.

Upon our return to the Castle, the footman informed me that tea would be served in the dining room at 4 o'clock. As only the Queen and Prince Philip were in residence, I simply expected a cuppa with a biscuit or two. How wrong I was. The dining table was fully laid for a sit-down tea. The Queen sat at one end of the table and Prince Philip at the other. The lady-in-waiting, the private secretary, the equerry and the deputy master of the household filled the remaining seats, and I was told to sit on the Queen's left.

There were no servants; this was a private affair and everyone had to fend for themselves, although the Queen did pour my tea. The walk had left me ravenous and the plates of sandwiches looked delicious, as did the array of cakes and biscuits. I politely held back, nibbling on a couple of rectangular egg and cucumber sandwiches and a slice of fruit cake. We chatted easily, while at our feet the corgis jockeyed for position in the hope that someone would miss their mouth. For fear of being bitten, I moved my feet only to hear a loud yelp. *Oh dear*, I thought. The Queen looked at me.

'Was that you?'

I don't know why it flashed into my mind, but I thought of Miss Piggy from *The Muppet Show*, and was about to say 'Moi?' I thought better of it, and respectfully said, 'No, Your Majesty, not me.'

I doubt she believed me, but she knew full well that the dogs could be a bit of a nuisance. After tea, we all went our separate ways. I went for another walk along the River Dee, which flowed through the estate. I was reminded of the photos taken of my new charges, the Prince and Princess of Wales, in that very same spot seven years earlier. Having just returned from their honeymoon aboard *Britannia*, they were so happy as they posed for the world's media.

While daytime was casual at Balmoral, black-tie was required for dinner. I returned to my room to find that my shirt and dinner suit had been neatly pressed and hung in the wardrobe. My bowtie, black shoes and socks had also been laid out.

Unlike the free-for-all nature of afternoon tea, there was a formal seating plan for dinner. Again, the Queen and Prince Philip sat at either end of the dining table, and

I returned to my seat on the Queen's left. The corgis were noticeably absent. Dinner lasted exactly 75 minutes before we adjourned for coffee in the drawing room. It was there that I took my leave and said goodbye to the Queen and Prince Philip, as I would be returning to London early the next day.

My brief visit to Balmoral was very special. The Queen was a marvellous host, especially given that I was one of her employees. It is customary for senior people joining the royal household to receive an audience with the Queen, their ultimate boss. Such meetings can take place at Buckingham Palace or Windsor Castle. That I was granted a 24-hour dine-and-sleep audience at her Scottish retreat was a gift I will never forget.

*

I had been no less excited in the summer of 1947, when told I was going to see my mother. Did she feel the same way about seeing me? I didn't know.

Being not quite seven years old, I had no idea how she would react upon being reunited or, indeed, how I would react to seeing her. In hindsight, I suspect our reunion was mostly down to the continual pressure placed on her by my aunt and uncles, who must have felt it a pretty poor state of affairs that they were left with the responsibility of her only child.

None of this occurred to me; I was only pleased and grateful that I was going to see her. My Aunt Ruth took me to a tea lounge just off Oxford Street in London, of which there were many back in those days. When I saw my mother I was struck by how young and beautiful she was.

By this time – I'm not sure how soon it was after she had left my father – she had acquired a new husband, Reg Arbiter, and moved to St John's Wood. I soon realised that Reg bore a more striking similarity to my headmaster than my late father. He was another one who liked his drink, and most of the time too much of it.

I had become a somewhat rootless child of no fixed abode, my only permanent address being that of my much-despised school. Spending time with my mother felt nothing like I had imagined it would for other normal children. While my school friends would skip off home on what were known as Visiting Sundays, my mother and Reg would take me to elegant pubs and restaurants: The Manor in Bracknell, the Compleat Angler in Marlow, Skindles in Maidenhead and the French Horn in Sonning, to name but a few. All very posh, all very elegant, all very expensive…and all very alien to a boy in short trousers. Here they would linger over a long lunch with the drink flowing while I, bored beyond tears, tried to amuse myself.

When I went to Holme Grange in January 1947 I was known as Richard Presch, my father's surname, and the name I was born with. By the time I reunited with my mother, she had taken her second husband's name, and went by Ruth Arbiter. Aged seven and still being bullied by the older boys and caned regularly by the headmaster, I was beginning to develop an independent streak. I was not willing to be the butt of the many cruel jokes any longer.

I confronted my mother and explained that it would be very odd and embarrassing for us to have different last names.

'Well, that's simple,' she said. 'We'll just tell the headmaster to change it'.

I'm not sure whether Reg was ever consulted, but overnight my name changed from Presch to Arbiter.

I never particularly liked my two given forenames, Richard and Winston. My mother was a great admirer of Winston Churchill, but the only thing I had in common with the famed prime minister is that we both flunked school. My mother said she liked Richard because, when shortened, it became 'Dickie'. She only addressed me as Richard when I had done something naughty.

I have been known as Dickie Arbiter throughout my life, although official documents all read Richard Winston Arbiter until I was in my 60s, when I finally got around to legally changing my name to Dickie, ditching Richard and Winston once and for all.

Once term ended, I went to live with my mother and Reg in their flat, sleeping on a pull-down bed in their bedroom. Although they were both out almost every night, it was hardly an ideal situation, and it was perhaps a blessing that this second marriage soon floundered. I for one wasn't sad when I learned that it was over, and that henceforth it would be just the two of us.

I was particularly happy when, at the start of the summer holidays in 1950, my mother collected me from Waterloo Station and announced that we were heading off to Rapallo, in Italy. I was almost ten years old when she introduced me to the high life – the kind of life my mother seemed to prefer. We travelled from Victoria Station on the boat train, then transferred at Calais to the elegantly named Blue Train, or Rome Express, where we overnighted in grand berths. I have no idea how she afforded it – much less the expensive ruby pendant and matching earrings I remember her buying – but she clearly had sufficient funds to feed her hunger for high-end-living. We were booked into the imposing Excelsior Hotel, where I had my first taste of real Russian caviar. It must have cost an absolute fortune, but I thought it was ghastly.

My mother had a friend there called Gianni. I remember him taking me out alone on his sailing yacht (my mother didn't go near sail boats) and being adrift at sea until three in the morning due to a lack of wind. No-one had considered the fact that I couldn't swim.

But I survived, and thrived, even though our arrangements were eccentric. Between that holiday and my leaving Holme Grange in the summer of 1951, I had lived under five or six different roofs. Where my mother lived when I was in school still remains a mystery.

I would have flourished anywhere once I finally left my boarding school, as apart from the sport – the only enjoyable aspect of the curriculum – I was profoundly glad to wave it all goodbye. I was equally miserable for a short time at St Martin in the Fields school in Trafalgar Square; the staff there had some crazy notion that a nice Jewish boy should be confirmed into the Church of England. But once I settled into Clark's College in Cricklewood, north

London – thanks yet again to Uncle Eric – I couldn't have been happier.

The only thing I really missed was the opportunity for sport. At Holme Grange, I relished both football and cricket, though I wasn't particularly brilliant at either. I also now realised that being able to play organized sport of some kind every day was a luxury. All that was on offer at Clark's College was a couple of hours a week; I was anxious to find a substitute.

We were living in Notting Hill Gate, in Kensington Park Gardens, and my mother had been giving my inactivity some thought. In her case, it was probably with a more prosaic ambition – to keep her suddenly very present son out of mischief. With Queens Ice Rink a mere bus or tube train ride away, she hit upon a plan.

'How would you like to try ice skating?'

Seeing how readily I took to the idea, she was very supportive of my new endeavour, even encouraging me to start taking lessons. This was thrilling, and when she said she would buy me my own boots, I couldn't have been more excited. No more wriggling my feet into the smelly, battered rink rentals. There was just one unfortunate detail – she thought I'd look best wearing white ones.

'I can't go in these!' I moaned, aghast, when she presented them to me. 'White boots are for girls. Boys wear black ones!'

But my mother wasn't one with whom to argue. I was given one choice – wear white boots or forget the whole thing. I realised I loved ice-skating more than life itself. I duly trooped down to Queens and reluctantly put them on, much to the amusement of my fellow junior skaters and the consternation of my lovely but formidable ice-skating teacher, Gladys Hogg.

Gladys was something of a celebrity at Queens, having been a pairs roller-skating champion in the 1920s and an ice-dancing champion in the 1930s. She was also notching up some success as a coach when I arrived. She had trained the brother and sister pair skating champions, John and Jennifer Nicks, and a couple who would go on to become European and World ice dance champions, Courtney Jones and June Markham (ice dance didn't become a Winter Olympic discipline until 1976). Perhaps her best-known prodigy was Olympic gold medalist, Robin Cousins.

Now she had me to lick into shape. 'Ah, Dickie,' she said, as I appeared on the ice, my beet-red face contrasting with the snowy leather on my feet. 'Are these *your* boots?' Stifling her guffaws, she added, 'I see. Well, well, how... erm...*nice.*'

I did what one would at that age, and burst into tears. As if that wasn't bad enough, the crying set off a second reaction – I wet myself, creating a yellow puddle on the ice beneath me.

After such a humiliating experience most would have abandoned the whole idea, but such was my love of the sport, I continued. Before long, my feet outgrew the hated white boots, and though I had no idea where the money came from, my mother gave me five £5 notes with which I was finally able to buy a pair of black skates.

I soon began learning to ice-dance with another brilliant teacher called Janet Smith, and by the time I was 13, I had put the whole Holme Grange nightmare behind me. I was going to the rink three or four times a week, sometimes more. I couldn't have been happier, but my mother's enthusiasm began to wane. What had begun as an activity to keep me occupied when not in school had become something of an obsession and, in my mother's eyes, not a healthy one. She grew increasingly concerned that I seemed to do nothing else, including my homework. She tried to have rink manager Harry Lauder ban me, but I had earned a free pass by sweeping the ice between sessions, and fortunately I was a favorite of his.

'Don't worry,' he told me. 'Let's put it this way. If I don't actually see you, I can't ban you. Get me?'

Needless to say, I became Queens' own Scarlet Pimpernel.

Sadly, the relative idyll of those years wasn't to last. As night follows day, so my GCE O-Level examinations followed after several years of academic diligence, but it appeared I wasn't going to be allowed to take mine.

I had always been a hard-working pupil at Clarks College. I was regularly in the top three in my class, and served as deputy captain of both the football and cricket teams. By my final year, I was also Head Boy. My only drawback was that I point-blank refused to do my homework. Not just because it ate into my skating time, but because I didn't believe it should be given at all. In my mind, when one left school for the day, that was it. Time out of school should be free.

Looking back, I am tickled by my commitment to this belief. I don't recall being particularly defiant, but there was clearly a streak of self-determination in there somewhere because I never bent in my resolve. As a result the headmaster informed my mother that it would be pointless for me to take any O' Levels. 'Your son is wasting our time and your money,' he said.

That was that. In April 1957, I was cut loose from school. When I awoke the following morning I lay in bed wondering what on earth would come next, but the period of freedom proved to be extremely short. Unbeknown to me, my mother had an uncle who lived in Southern Rhodesia. Quite out of the blue, he sent us two tickets with an invitation to visit him for a holiday. Again this was 1957, another age in terms of travel. No-one in his right mind travelled 6,000 miles just to take a holiday, even to a place he really wanted to see.

And I didn't want to see Southern Rhodesia. Though I had left school, I had no wish to travel. I had my friends and I had my skating. I certainly had no inclination to visit what was then generally described as 'darkest' Africa.

My mother wrote to my great-uncle explaining that she was grateful for the offer, but that our coming to visit was out of the question. I was wrong to assume that that was the end of it. I have no idea what else she wrote in that letter, but a month or so later, she called me to her.

'Dickie…' she said, in a tone usually reserved for when I had done something wrong.

'Yes?'

'It's Uncle Walter in Rhodesia…'

'Yes?'

Were we going on holiday to darkest Africa after all?

Apparently not. Not for a holiday, anyway.

'Well,' she continued, 'he's written back and suggested we go out there to *live*. And after *much* consideration, I have agreed. He's sending us two sea passages. In the meantime there is a lot to do because we have to apply for residency.'

She had lost me on 'live'. I didn't want to live in darkest Africa. I wanted to stay in London. How could she agree to something like that? I was 16. Did she not think to consult me?

It would be a while before the ramifications of such a move began to sink in, but for the moment I felt nothing but outrage. I knew better than to question her, so I just pushed off to the ice rink.

We were emigrating to Bulawayo, the second largest city in Southern Rhodesia. Once I recovered from the shock, I became both excited and disappointed. Disappointed because it meant I would now have to give up my beloved ice-skating; I didn't imagine they had ice rinks on the African continent. At the same time a delicious feeling of anticipation began to settle in. Being rootless meant there was no sense of ties being severed…and I have been criss-crossing the globe ever since.

CHAPTER 4

A Bite of the Big Apple

February 1989

The Royal Family spends a large part of its year conducting engagements. As a press secretary with responsibility to the Prince and Princess of Wales, I knew my job would be as peripatetic as it had been for all of my working life.

It would take me to places I never imagined I'd go. Now, my first overseas trip with a member of 'The Firm' would have me accompanying Diana on an official royal tour to New York.

I was already a seasoned traveler, but I had never traveled like this. As I packed my dinner jacket on the eve of my flight to JFK, I felt like a novice. This time around I would not be a part of the media scrum, but rather serving as a courtier attending to my principal. At the same time, I would be required to play the media game, ensuring that the press saw all that I had organized.

I had been to Canada several times, but never to the US. The Princess of Wales's first solo visit abroad was to

Oslo in 1984, but her first solo tour was a first for me too. The time had come for me to put into practice all that I had learned with regard to the planning of royal tours.

And they did take a lot of planning. Overseas tours don't just begin upon arrival. Months of preparation are involved from the time an invitation to visit a country is received. Dates, itineraries and accommodation all have to be arranged ahead of time.

All royal engagements require some degree of reconnoitre prior to the event. In the case of overseas visits, a small team, usually led by the private secretary – who reports to the particular royal involved – heads out on a 'recce'. Accompanying him or her is an equerry – a member of the Army, Royal Navy or Royal Air Force. The equerry is generally on a two-and-a-half year secondment to the Royal Family, and is charged with overseeing all of the logistics.

Next up is the PPO (Personal Protection Officer), whose job it is to liaise with the local police regarding security. Finally, there was my role as press secretary, which was to ensure that both the UK and the host country's media covered the event with minimal disruption.

It is a multi-faceted role. I arranged hotels for the media, and if the tour was moving across country I organized transportation between locales. Ground and air transportation was planned with the assistance of our Embassy or High Commission. Air travel was always charged to the individual UK media outlets, not the public purse. I would then send out an advisory note to all the media organisations, which would allow journalists, broadcasters and photographers to decide whom they wanted to send on the tour.

With so much experience on the other side of the fence, giving the media what I knew they wanted felt instinctive. I loved the organisational aspect of a royal visit. It was very satisfying to see it all come together. By nature the media is never fully content with what it is provided, but it was always satisfying to see the pack reasonably satisfied.

Recces were tightly conducted. There was no slack, and they were never longer than the proposed visit itself. A four-day tour meant no more than a four-day recce. They were also fine examples of diplomacy in action. We always worked alongside our own embassy or High Commission and with representatives from the host country's Ministry of Foreign Affairs, or, in the case of New York City, the State Department.

That said, we didn't actually do the recce for the Princess's first solo trip to New York. Diana's private secretary, Anne Beckwith-Smith, undertook it the previous December in order to kill two birds with one stone. Along with Diana's PPO, Anne was going to recce Necker Island (Richard Branson's private island), for a proposed holiday with William and Harry, which Diana was planning to take immediately after her visit to New York.

Press secretaries didn't recce private visits. Private meant private, and as we were paid by the civil list, we weren't allowed to undertake any unofficial duties. Holidays such as this were strictly off limits. I didn't necessarily agree. Private it might have been, but as the Princess was to learn, had there been a press secretary on hand to manage the hordes of press that descended upon Necker, her holiday might have been significantly more private than it was. Instead, the papers were filled with pages of grainy pictures taken by photographers bobbing in boats a hundred metres off shore for the duration of her break with the boys.

It was strange to be packing for New York's sub-zero temperatures, as I had only just returned from a recce in the sweltering heat of the Gulf 48 hours earlier. I'd been doing the groundwork for a forthcoming joint visit by the Prince and Princess to Kuwait, Bahrain and the United Arab Emirates.

Coming from the temperatures of 40°C back to the UK was shock enough. Now I'd be heading straight into the brutal New York winter, two days in advance of the Princess.

Diana travelled on Concorde, which meant that she'd touch down in New York earlier than she had left London. Our team, including Graham Smith, her lead protection officer, and Lieutenant Commander Patrick Jephson, her equerry, flew in on a British Airways 747. Along with the State Department and the New York Police Department (NYPD) – who would be in charge of convoys – our task was to revisit all of the venues that would be hosting the Princess before she arrived.

While we weren't royal ourselves, we did enjoy many royal privileges. The length of American immigration queues was legendary, but there was to be no standing in line for us. State Department officials, along with Sally

O'Brien from our Washington Embassy, met us at the gate and whisked us through the airport. It was left to a British Consulate official to get the appropriate entry stamps in our passports and transport our luggage to the five-star Hotel Plaza Athenée on East 64th Street. Free of baggage concerns we had only to be responsible for ourselves and the clothes on our backs.

New York certainly lived up to its reputation. I was so excited that it was all I could do not to stick my head out of the window and burst into song. I expect my colleagues were immensely grateful that I didn't.

Long haul travel had become the norm for me, but for the Princess, the 1989 visit to New York was going to be something of a milestone. While she was a well-travelled royal by this point, the tour was to be her first solo engagement outside the UK. The eyes of the world would be upon her to see how she would cope. Everyone may have had an opinion about her, but for most, the information was gathered second hand.

I had had a chance to get to know her, and in doing so began to understand the kind of person she was. In a word, she was complicated. If things were going her way, she was fine. If anything out of the ordinary occurred – anything that conflicted with what she wanted to do, and in *her* way – then you were frozen out and left to stew until she decided to invite you back into the fold. The freeze could last days or even weeks, and no-one was immune.

I was subjected to one or two myself.

When Patrick Jephson was invited to serve as Diana's Private Secretary, after completing his two-and-a-half-year stint as her Equerry, she decided that she wanted to hold a weekly programme meeting with him and me. On one occasion Patrick warned me that the Princess was hoping to arrange a reception at Kensington Palace for the England football team.

'Why?,' I asked. 'They lost their recent game.'

Agreeing, he replied, 'Then why don't *you* tell her that, Dickie? It would be better coming from you.'

As her private secretary, Patrick needed to keep her on side. It didn't matter if she froze out the press secretary.

'Okay, Patrick,' I said. 'But you know what'll happen. She'll sulk and won't speak to me until she wants something.'

Moments later, the Princess walked into Patrick's office. We discussed the events of the previous week as well as what was to come.

It was then that Patrick said to Diana, 'Wasn't there something you wanted to ask Dickie, Ma'am?'

Thanks a bundle, Patrick.

'Dickie,' Diana said, 'I want to host a reception for the England football team. What do you think?'

'It's a lovely idea, Ma'am, but why? They lost. If you go ahead, then you'll have to give one to the cricket team, the equestrian team, the hockey team, the rugby team, the list is endless.' I continued, not willing to let her get a word in, 'No, Ma'am, it just won't work.'

'Yes, I see what you mean,' she said.

With that, the meeting was over.

Patrick smiled…and I didn't hear from Diana again for the next two weeks.

Eventually, I learned not to take the freezes personally, but during those early days, I was on the same learning curve as everyone else.

That is not to say that she was any less engaging or fun to be with. This solo trip was a chance to see her in action first hand. From the minute she stepped off the plane, I recognised how much of a natural she was, and how much potential she had as a roving ambassador for the UK. She was a true professional – warm, approachable and incredibly charismatic. It was as if she'd been doing it all her life.

The tour began in downtown Manhattan. I had spent the better part of the day with the media, ensuring that the British press had been given the right positions. I was also on hand to brief HRH (Her Royal Highness) of any untoward changes to the itinerary. I tended to stick with the media, believing I could best do my job in the thick of the press pack, as opposed to loitering with the strap-hangers traipsing along with the royal party.

Not that I minded traipsing along with the royal party when it was required. The NYPD handled our motorcade. Travelling in such a convoy was a mind-blowing experience. Not since my national service had I seen so many guns. As our motorcade progressed through the cavernous city streets, menacing secret service SWAT teams scoured the rooftops while those escorting us on the ground jumped out of their blacked-out SUVs at each red light. It was the New York of my every childhood imagining.

As everyone expected, the Princess was off to an excellent start. America really took to her. She was soon to seal her position as the country's favourite and most famous royal.

The trip included a visit to the Henry Street Day Care Center on the Lower East Side, one of the city's poorest areas. She also met a group of children suffering from AIDS in the pediatric ward at Harlem Hospital. At the time AIDS was still greatly misunderstood. It was therefore sure to be a high-profile visit, and we were concerned about how it might go. The head of the unit, a no-nonsense, outspoken Dr. Margaret Haegarty, was of Irish descent, and known for her republican sympathies. Regardless, Diana was masterful when it came to exploding the then-famous 'do not touch' myth.

We needn't have worried. There was no sense of antagonism towards the monarchy. Far from it. When asked by the Princess if Americans were educated about AIDS, Dr Haegarty's reply was as pleasing as it was unexpected. 'Our own royalty,' she said, 'whatever that is – being a democracy or a republic or whatever – hasn't done anything nearly as symbolic as what you have done here today.'

There was no finer endorsement of the Princess's visit, and we heaved a collective sigh of relief.

I have always loved flying, so travelling home with the Princess on Concorde was the icing on the cake of what had been a high-profile and extremely successful visit. She'd impressed me greatly, though perhaps I should have expected that things would pan out as well as they did. As a reporter I had been at the Middlesex Hospital in Central London two years earlier when, upon opening an AIDS ward and meeting patients with Professor Michael Adler, Diana had offered her hand to an afflicted patient. It was an enormously significant story at the time, and despite a broad Department of Health campaign to educate the public, it was still widely believed that you could catch AIDS via touch alone. Diana's gesture resulted in a major break-through in public perception. Now, in New York, she had done it again. No wonder she became America's sweetheart.

No sooner had we returned from our triumphant trip to New York than it was time to depart for my first joint tour with the Prince and Princess. In March of 1989, the couple embarked on a visit to the Gulf making stops in Kuwait, Bahrain, Abu Dhabi and Dubai. My foremost memory of the visit, however, is one of overwhelming heat. Little did I know at the time how much excessive heat was going to play a factor in our future royal tours. I thought I had experienced the most extreme temperatures when I was in the army, patrolling the Zambezi Valley during my days in Rhodesia, but Kuwait was like walking into a blast furnace, the only saving graces being the air-conditioned car ride to the air-conditioned venue, before retreating back to the comfort of the air-conditioned car.

The Gulf tour went incredibly well. The Prince and Princess said all the right things, shook all the right hands and visited all the right places. But it was in the United Arab Emirates that we experienced the most unbelievable hospitality. We were invited to attend a sit down picnic lunch beneath the wafty ceiling of a Bedouin tent in an oasis just outside Abu Dhabi. Unlike my picnic at Balmoral seven months previously, where we had sat inside a log cabin as it rained continuously outside, this was opulent in the extreme. A feast of delicacies the likes of which I had only ever seen in the movies was spread before us. Sadly, I was soon put off my food when a bowl brimming with steaming sheep eyes was placed in front of me. All I could think of was poor Larry the Lamb. Following lunch the Prince and Princess spent the afternoon watching camel racing. It's a popular sport in the Middle East with jockeys, usually small boys, perched precariously atop their steeds. I had seen camels run in the movie *Lawrence of Arabia*, but it is only upon seeing them in the flesh that one realises just how fast they are.

The final day of the Gulf tour concluded with a dinner hosted by the ruler, Sheikh Maktoum. The Prince was flying on to Saudi Arabia in the morning, while the Princess was due to travel home that night on a scheduled British Airways flight. At dinner we received word that that the BA flight was delayed in Hong Kong and wouldn't reach Dubai until 5am. Without so much as a pause for breath, Sheikh Hamdan, Dubai's deputy ruler, said, 'Take my plane. It is crewed 24/7 and ready to fly anywhere at a moment's notice.' We were all taken aback by his generous offer, but none more so than the Princess, who had had enough of the heat and was eager to get home to 'her boys'. We assumed the jumbo jet would be configured with the standard layout. The Princess would sit in First Class, and those of us accompanying her, five in total, would travel in Business Class. Instead, the plane that greeted us gave new meaning to the phrase *traveling in style*. The rear of the aircraft did indeed have conventional seating, but the middle section comprised three double bedrooms with en suite shower facilities. The front of the plane was a *Majlis* – the Arabic word meaning a place for sitting. Finally, the upper deck was arranged as a lounge, with low coffee tables that rose up to form a full dining table. Once we had reached our cruising altitude of 45,000 feet, dinner was served.

At 4:45am we roared into London's Heathrow Airport in the lap of luxury. With cars awaiting our arrival on the apron, the Princess was whisked off to Kensington Palace, getting her home with plenty of time to spare before her boys woke up.

CHAPTER 5

The Myth-busting Princess

November 1989

M y first year in the Royal Household flew by in a haze of activity. We arranged every tour schedule two to three months in advance, which required a lot of pre-tour organization and administration, as well as two roundtrips to each country – once for the recce, and then again two months later for the tour itself.

Following Diana's solo trip to New York, we had two further overseas tours, this time involving both Charles and Diana. By the end of that year, I had notched up seven overseas trips, travelling once to New York and twice to the Gulf, Indonesia and Hong Kong respectively. I was in my element, though my suitcase was taking a battering.

*

May 1957 saw the beginning of my adventure to the African continent, and the beginning of a wanderlust that I never relinquished. My mother, then 36, and I set off by train from London's Waterloo station, she looking glamorous in a sharp tailored skirt suit, and I in grey flannels, blazer and tie. In those days one always dressed formally when travelling; T-shirts and trainers were not yet in fashion and as such were strictly reserved for the playing fields.

I had resigned myself to departing England's shores for a life on a continent that seemed a million miles away. Being 16, I was excited by the adventure of it all, which helped quell my natural teenage anxieties.

Over the course of almost three weeks our journey would take us around the coast of Africa to Durban, but I was perplexed by a number of questions: What did one do at sea for all that time? Was there entertainment? Would there be anyone else my age, and uppermost in my mind, would there be girls on board? The issue of quite what I was going to do once we arrived in Rhodesia didn't even enter my thinking; all I could see was three weeks of playtime ahead, and I fully intended to make the most of it.

The train took us to Southampton, a bustling seaport with ships of every conceivable size from all over the world loading and unloading their cargo. There were ocean-going liners awaiting passengers, civil servants heading off to colonial postings and migrants setting off to begin a new life on distant shores. It was a different era – a time in which Great Britain still had her colonies and exported not only goods, but also people. Those emigrating represented a chance to live a different kind of life in decidedly less inclement surroundings. Ocean cruising simply for the sake of a luxury vacation would not become mainstream for several years.

My mother and I fell into the migrant category,

travelling aboard the Union-Castle Line's *Athlone Castle* –
a modest ship of a little under 26,000 tonnes – to begin
our new life in Southern Rhodesia. The journey from
Southampton to Cape Town took 13 days, but it was not
our final port of disembarkation. We still had to sail an
additional four days around the Cape, stopping off at
Port Elizabeth and East London before reaching our desti-
nation, Durban.

The journey was not without incident. We sailed
through the infamous Cape Rollers – waves that can reach
dizzying heights in excess of 40 feet. For a ship with no
stabilizers, it left nothing to the imagination as we rocked
and rolled on the high seas.

Otherwise life on board was fairly soporific. An endless
round of sunbathing, eating and drinking by day, followed
by nights that involved more of the same, with the only
difference being that dancing replaced sunbathing. As we
neared Cape Town, the end of the line for some, there was
a final flurry of excitement when it was announced that
there would be a last night fancy dress party.

In contrast to the generally low-key approach to leisure
time, which had prevailed up until that point, there was
suddenly an outpouring of competitive creative genius.
Everyone was keen to impress, and the talk turned to
whom would come dressed as what.

My mother had made several firm friends while
onboard, not difficult to do as a glamorous single woman,
and certainly not within the close confines of a ship at sea.
She had chosen her friendships wisely, for on the evening
of the party three imaginative young men in her group

appeared with some handy props in the form of what was apparently the ship's entire stock of black crepe paper with which they fashioned some show-stopping costumes. The three men dressed as nuns; I borrowed a cabin steward's tunic, and my mother appeared in a short negligee, a bra and five pairs of panties.

There was a method to this madness. As a steward I carried a tray on which were set bottles of gin and tonic and a propped-up envelope reading 'ship's issue'. Together we had entered the competition as 'the captain's nightcap,' and although we didn't win first prize, we certainly raised a few laughs – not least from the captain, who was one of the judges.

That night wasn't just an introduction into the ways in which adults make their own entertainment at sea. It was also the occasion of my first proper drink. At 16½ I had tried a thimbleful of watered-down wine many times, but I had never had a proper adult-sized drink. Bobbing around somewhere in the Atlantic Ocean with land a million miles away, I threw caution to the wind and accepted my first beer. I didn't particularly like it but, with no duty to pay, at least it was cheap. Where the gin and tonic ended up I have no idea.

They say all good things must come to an end. Any notion I might have had that this would be something of an extended holiday was sadly and quickly disabused.

Having taken no exams, I had no qualifications, and therefore immediately became the subject of intense family discussions. A path was set for me. I would commence an apprenticeship, and spend the next five years training to be an electrician. I had no say in the matter. It had all been arranged. My mother's Uncle Walter had used one of his contacts to get me a job in what was the country's largest electrical engineering firm. He took me for an interview with the owner and the foreman under whom I would be working. I was shown around the factory – a blur of grease, oil, loud noise and stares at the skinny Englishman. I was told to report the next day at 8am sharp.

Although I began my apprenticeship within days of arriving in Bulawayo, I found it incredibly difficult to establish friendships there. I was 17, and had not been schooled there, so meeting people wasn't easy. I joined Queens Sports Club and tried playing football, but with winter daytime temperatures of 25°C, I soon realised it was not for me, and despite the heat, cricket was not played during the winter months. Life in 1950s Rhodesia revolved around work, sport, the club bar and home. Adjusting to my new existence was very challenging and, tragically, five months after we arrived, Uncle Walter died. He had been rushed to hospital with suspected appendicitis. Two days after his operation, he collapsed in the bathroom and died of a massive heart attack. My mother was devastated, having shared so little time with him since their parting in Germany in 1934.

My saving grace during those trying times came in the form of a newspaper advertisement announcing auditions for an upcoming production of the Rogers and Hammerstein musical, *Oklahoma!* I was offered a place in the chorus. The only downside to the amateur production was the ten week rehearsal period for only one week of performance. I was crushed when the final curtain fell.

There was one major aspect to living in Southern Rhodesia that had never been explained to me. The country was just one of the three that made up the Federation of Rhodesia and Nyasaland – Northern Rhodesia (now Zambia), Nyasaland (now Malawi) and Southern Rhodesia (now Zimbabwe). All were under the umbrella of the federal government, with a governor in each of the three countries and a governor general overseeing all of them. It was one of those 'blue sky' ideas cooked up by the Colonial Office in London in 1950. It was doomed to failure and lasted precisely ten years from 1953 to 1963.

If the idea of a federation with so many governors was confusing to an outsider, then the idea of Southern Rhodesia – the only country within the federation to have had its own internal self-government and parliament since 1923 – was even more confusing. It's no wonder there were undercurrents of unrest amongst the indigenous population.

Social unrest requires government action and as a result, every white male over the age of 18 who had completed his education was required to do national service. A university course was the only exemption, and even that was temporary. Conscientious objectors were recommended to do their national service or conscientiously object from the inside of a prison cell.

This left me in a dispiriting situation. I had just left the United Kingdom, where national service was being phased out. Had I stayed, given my age, I would have escaped it. Now I had arrived in a country which for a period of time required me to do national service.

I have always believed that if one is required to do something and has no choice in the matter, then the best thing to do is to make the most of it and enjoy it. I don't doubt that my early experience at boarding school informed my way of thinking, but when it came to tough regimes – and national service in Rhodesia was certainly that – I already had the mental tools to cope.

Llewellyn Barracks, 12 miles north of Bulawayo, had previously been an RAF (Royal Air Force) pilot training camp during World War II, so it already had the infra-structure for military training. It was here that I went to do my army training with the Royal Rhodesia Regiment in the winter of 1959. Despite this being Africa, it really felt like winter, with nighttime temperatures dropping well below freezing. When I arrived the camp was under-going renovation, which meant that none of the barracks had heating or hot water. Each day dawned with the rude awakening of a cold shower.

Things didn't improve much after that. There was little time off in the army. The daily routine of weapons training, drill and PT (Physical Training) saw to that. The staff instructors always took a sadistic delight in finding something for us to do. Often this something stretched well into the night. Top of their to-do list was a full kit inspection in which everything had to be laid out perfectly on our beds. Even if you thought it was correct (and it generally was), they invariably didn't think so, and revealed their displeasure by tossing over your bed, spilling everything across the barrack room floor.

There was rarely any respite from full kit inspections. The same routine was repeated over and over until the instructors got bored and went off to annoy someone else. When we did have downtime it was spent well away from the barracks, hoisting beers in the canteen, putting the world to rights and playing snooker. The more talented among us provided the accompaniment by bashing out music on makeshift instruments.

We managed to find entertainment in the great outdoors if we were overnighting in the bush on exercise. While not quite in the mould of David Attenborough, we would often go out hunting for spiders and scorpions, put them under a glass jar and take bets on which would annihilate the other first.

The victor's prize was its freedom. We could only wait impatiently for our own.

As a glamorous 36-year-old new arrival to Bulawayo, my mother was pursued relentlessly and never short of a date. But it wasn't long before one man in particular stole her heart. He was a widower, who had sadly lost his wife as she gave birth to their third child. He never really got over it and dealt with his grief by drinking heavily.

He proposed to my mother within weeks of their meeting. She accepted, but on the condition that he give up alcohol altogether. He conceded, and never drank another drop. In January, 1958, eight months after arriving in Rhodesia, my mother became Mrs Asher Bernstein.

Asher, who ran a successful retail furniture business, was a tough, no-nonsense South African who had played rugby and cricket. At one time, he managed the Rhodesia Cricket Team on tour, and served on the Rhodesian Rugby Board. When his playing days ended, sport administration remained very much in his blood.

Never one to sit around, my mother always worked… not because she had to, but because she wanted to. Given her experience with one of the largest dress manufactures in London, she secured a job as a fashion buyer with Edgars, a South African retail outlet that was beginning to get a foothold in Rhodesia. The company is still there today, although now it is a fully owned Zimbabwean subsidiary. She remained with the company until her retirement in 1984.

Her marriage to Asher lasted until she was widowed in 1994. Currently a strong and robust woman of 93, she still lives in Bulawayo – a proud mother, grandmother and great-grandmother.

Through my work in the theatre I gathered a small circle of friends. Together we developed a New Year's Eve tradition. After midnight we would jump into our cars, a little worse for wear, and drive 22 miles outside of Bulawayo to the Matopos Hills. There we would watch the sun rise over the grave of Rhodesia's founder, Cecil John Rhodes.

Following my return to the UK in 1974, I went back to Bulawayo as often as possible in the ensuing years. It gave my daughter, Victoria, an opportunity to spend time with her grandparents, whom she adored.

My one sadness about our move to Rhodesia was that I never did see Uncle Eric again. He was a good man that life had dealt a bad hand.

*

It is sometimes assumed that the Royal Family's programme of global travel is instigated by and for them. Nothing could be further from the truth. Overseas visits don't happen because a member of the Royal Family fancies visiting one place or another. They come about in order to meet the needs and wants of the government according to current diplomatic relations, to promote British exports, or as part of a programme of cultural or educational exchanges. At times they are scheduled simply for the strategic importance of a particular country within its region.

Once a tour has been suggested, the next step is to approach a senior member of the Royal Family with a view to their undertaking a tour on behalf of 'UK plc'.

Only then is an invitation issued by the host country's head of state and plans drawn up for what the visit should entail. Getting the right programme mix is always a challenge for the private secretary. Such an invitation marks the start of intense negotiations. Their Royal Highnesses' private office will suggest certain events or locations. The British Ambassador will put forth his own list of proposals that the British Government would like for the royal in question to do. Finally, the host country's Ministry of Foreign Affairs will push for the inclusion of its own 'must sees and dos' in order to best present its country to the world's press.

The planning stage is a little like an extended game of poker, involving tactics, gamesmanship, fierce negotiation and, inevitably, winners and losers. At the same time, there's honour among all sides. When one concedes something, he generally gets something in return.

Sensibly, the royals stay out of this process until the point when they see the proposed programme. Then it is up to the private secretary to explain to whichever principal why certain events have been included. That done and agreed upon, the Royals themselves take centre stage. Once the day of the visit dawns, it's show time.

Given the various motivations involved in doing them, royal visits abroad generally necessitate a protracted and strategic dance. The 1989 visit to Indonesia – primarily taking place to boost exports there from the UK – was no exception. Once the rough outline was agreed upon, the tour leader, private secretary David Wright, would use all of the diplomatic skills at his disposal to finally present the proposed programme to the Prince and Princess. Though it was they who would ultimately sign off on the proposal, there was the usual input from both the Foreign Office and the host country, which weren't always of similar mind.

The private secretary that leads foreign visits is always a secondee from the Foreign Office, with a clear remit in terms of the interests of the UK. For this tour we were in the capable hands of David Wright. His diplomatic skills were much needed as well, because for months our ambassador in Jakarta had been trying to arrange a conference between British weapons manufacturers and

Indonesia's defense ministry and military – an attempt to boost British arms sales. The Indonesians, however, were lukewarm to any such arms conference, regardless of the dangled carrot that was the 'The Prince and Princess of Wales'.

There was much to be decided, and during the four-day recce we visited a number of options which, at least in principle, would work for all three interested parties. The royal couple would experience the country's culture on the island of Java, with a visit to the 9th century Mahāyāna Buddhist temple at Borobudur. The environment would be addressed with the inauguration of a desperately needed water purification plant. In acknowledgment of Indonesian tradition, a wreath would be laid at the Commonwealth War Graves Cemetery. There would be a visit to Jakarta's Sitanala leprosy hospital, and finally, trade talks would be discussed at reception at which the Prince would give a keynote speech.

After four hectic days and much debate and glad-handing, we left Jakarta with the understanding that we had an acceptable programme. What we didn't know (and were only to discover when the equerry, Lt Commander Patrick Jephson and I returned two days in advance of the royal visit) was that President Suharto wasn't pleased with the agreed upon programme which, it turned out, he had only seen a few days prior to the Prince and Princess's arrival.

He was therefore very keen to change it. He made it clear to us that he didn't like the idea of the Princess going to the leprosy hospital, in particular. 'Why would she want to go and see lots of sick people' he wanted to know, 'when she could visit the Taman Mini cultural park or – much more her thing – go to a fashion show?'

The Princess's interests and passions aside – all of which we knew well – it soon became obvious that Taman Mini was Mrs Suharto's pet project. Self-serving interests were undoubtedly being put into play. This might also have been a factor in his displeasure at the Prince visiting the water purification plant, as it was based in an overcrowded shanty-town.

Patrick Jephson, an excellent naval officer, which might account for his unflappability, did what he was best at in the face of last-minute programme changes – found solutions that would satisfy everyone. Thousands of miles away from his seniors at St James's Palace, he tweaked the programme just enough to hopefully calm the president and keep everyone else happy. The Prince and Princess *would* go to Taman Mini, with the understanding that she could still visit the Sitanala leprosy hospital. The Prince *would* personally inaugurate the British-designed water purification plant. After all, the plant made stagnant, undrinkable water safe while also providing electricity for 6,000 villages, all of which would surely present the President in the best possible light.

Still, Suharto objected, primarily to the suggestion of the Prince visiting a shanty-town – a place he felt no Prince should go. But Patrick dug in his heels and insisted that this, being an environmental project, was of great personal interest to His Royal Highness...not to mention a benefit to the community.

The Indonesians reluctantly relented and, as we were to find out, at great cost. When we arrived at the location for a final check before His Royal Highness's arrival, we found a dusty track which connected to a stagnant, heavily polluted canal brimful of general and human waste and with the occasional dead animal floating by.

This was reality. We could live with it. We certainly knew it wouldn't faze His Royal Highness. But, as it turned out, it wouldn't have mattered anyway. Scant hours before the visit, the Indonesians dredged the canal till the water ran clear and without flotsam. They had also covered the entire track with granite chippings.

We subsequently learned that within an hour of Charles's departure, the garbage was back floating its merry way down the canal and every last chip of granite had disappeared. This sort of cosmetic treatment was nothing new to us. There were few royal visits, even in the UK, that weren't preceded by a hasty coat of paint.

Every day was hot and steamy in Jakarta, but the day the Princess visited the Sitanala leprosy hospital was particularly oppressive. Temperatures had topped 30°C, and with 90 percent humidity, the air was dripping.

Despite the heat, the hospital felt bright and at least reasonably airy, in part because there were windows stretching the full length of the ward. Well, at least there were spaces where windows would have been. As it was they were glassless, giving the press gathered outside an unrestricted view of the Princess at work, and the opportunity to stick their lenses through the openings in a gesture which, in any other circumstance, might have felt intrusive.

The photographers didn't appear to bother the patients, and they certainly didn't deter Her Royal Highness. The Princess of 1989 was a very different woman from the gauche 19-year-old to whom Charles had proposed. Now in her late 20s, and a capable and clearly devoted mother to two young sons, she'd grown significantly in stature and confidence. She'd carved out for herself a role as a dedicated charity supporter and become, arguably, the first member of the Royal Family to really connect with the people.

It was a role that would come to define her – warm where Charles was reticent, hands-on where he was perceived to be mostly hands-off. Doing away with the traditional codes of behavior, Diana was seen to be a breath of fresh air in what had begun to be viewed as a somewhat stuffy institution.

Most of this perception was inaccurate and based on speculation rather than fact. The speculation grew out of an understanding that there were certain fixed rules about how we mere mortals could and should behave around the Royal Family. I began covering the royals as a reporter in 1977, at the time of the Queen's silver jubilee. One of the first things I learned was that, contrary to popular opinion, no such obligatory rules actually existed.

Not as any sort of law, anyway. Mostly they were made up by courtiers over the centuries, and retained for whatever reason. Regardless, what may have befitted the social mores of the 18th or 19th centuries wasn't necessarily right for modern times. Bowing or curtseying when in the presence of a member of the Royal Family? Not necessary. Not unless one chooses to.

Don't address the Queen until she addresses you? On the contrary. In fact, that misconception is possibly responsible for Her Majesty being lampooned from time to time for asking seemingly bland questions like 'where do you come from?' or 'have you been waiting long?' But what else is she to do? When faced with silence someone has to break the ice, after all. The Queen knows full well from experience that if she starts a conversation, people won't feel so intimidated around her.

The only obligatory rule is that, in the first instance, one is to address the Queen as 'Your Majesty'. Thereafter it is permissible to call her 'Ma'am' (rhyming with jam). Other members of the Royal Family – male and female – are firstly referred to as 'Your Royal Highness' and thereafter as Sir or Ma'am, as well.

Nothing officially changed when Lady Diana Spencer became the Princess of Wales, but there was a sense with the populous that she did things differently – that she was connected to the regular folk in a way unlike those born royal. Whether there was any truth to that is difficult to say. I'm tempted to suggest that it was as much about her youth and beauty as anything, but there was no doubt that she had a way of connecting that felt fresh, and unquestionably groundbreaking for the period.

Both as a mother and an official member of the Royal Family, Diana had seen and experienced more than most young women her age. Whatever the Waleses marital situation was behind closed doors, in public she was a consummate professional, working hard at the complex job life had landed her. Taking on the challenges of touring seemed second nature to her, which I was now witnessing first hand.

If AIDS patients were seen as modern-day lepers, then here in Indonesia were the real thing. Anyone not medically minded could have been forgiven for accepting the age-old folklore about the risk of getting too close to them physically. As ever, Diana strode onto the ward without a second thought. She would sit among the patients, shaking hands and holding stumps where hands had once been.

She was always keen to get close to those she was visiting, often chatting to people at length with genuine interest. It was a gesture which greatly pleased both the Indonesian officials present, as well as The Leprosy Mission back in the UK – a charity for which the Princess subsequently became patron.

As was the case with Diana's visit to AIDS patients at Middlesex Hospital three years prior, pictures conveyed a message more powerfully than words ever could.

CHAPTER 6

An Iron Curtain Call

May 1990

The spring of 1990 saw another royal first, as the Prince and Princess of Wales made their way east for the first official royal visit to Hungary. A former Warsaw Pact country, Hungary was undergoing a time of great political change. The first democratic elections had been held just a month prior. It would be a very different place to that which the Duke of Edinburgh had visited in 1978 and 1984, to compete in the World Carriage Driving Championships.

I had been to a number of countries on the European continent, but never to a communist – or even former communist – country. I knew it would be a fascinating glimpse into a part of the world that had previously been a mystery to the west. It was also another opportunity for the Princess to demonstrate what a positive asset she had become to 'the firm'.

President-elect Árpád Göncz and his visibly nervous wife Maria met Charles and Diana upon their arrival in Budapest. As the Prince inspected the honour guard alongside the President, I noted that the Princess had also sensed Mrs Göncz unease. From my position next to the press pen I watched as Diana, in an unprecedented move for a member of the Royal Family, took Mrs Göncz's hand, and continued to hold it as the two women walked down the red carpet.

She was without question becoming a star.

*

My own ambitions for stardom began early. I had caught the acting bug at prep school where, due to my diminutive stature and my slightly 'pretty boy' looks, I was regularly cast as a girl in our various school productions. I didn't object to this. All I wanted was to be on the stage, and it was a pull that was never to leave me.

Rhodesia, in that respect, had been kind to me. Yes, I had to toil at my apprenticeship and national service, but I began doing amateur dramatics when my schedule allowed. By the time I was a fully qualified electrician, I had already decided to discard my tools, and travel to Johannesburg to seek fame and fortune.

Johannesburg turned out to be rather different from my expectations. As I knew no-one, apart from a great-aunt and great-uncle who kindly agreed to put me up for a few days on a settee in their dining room, I needed to hit the ground running. I had to find a place to call home, and more importantly, find a way to earn a living.

Through the grapevine I had heard of a place called the Alba Hotel, and made it my first port of call. It was located in Braamfontein, a central suburb of Johannesburg that attracted budding thespians. Anyone who worked in theatre seemed to gravitate towards the area, and I decided I could do worse than make it my plan as well. Luckily I managed to find work quickly. It may have been for very little money and absolutely no fame, but it was a step on the ladder, and I was happy to have made the first rung. I worked throughout the country, taking on various roles. I assistant-stage-managed Chekov's *The Cherry Orchard* for the Performing Arts Council Transvaal. I toured, performing onstage, in the Rogers and Hammerstein musical *The King and I*. I played the lead in Anne Nichols's 1920s play *Abie's Irish Rose* and I worked behind the scenes stage-directing *The Adam Leslie Revue,* which started with a six-month run in Johannesburg before going on tour to Durban, Port Elizabeth, Cape Town, Bloemfointein and Peitersburg in South Africa. The show played in Bulawayo, Rhodesia, closing in Johannesburg after a three-month run.

Looking back, it doesn't seem like a lot, but I was having the time of my life. I was in my element, and more importantly, continuously employed for two and a half years in what has always been a precarious industry.

By 1965, however, I had a new plan – to return to the UK. For some reason I had been increasingly feeling the tug of home. I headed back, keen to make my contribution to the swinging 60s, which were by now in full swing.

Again I fell on my feet, landing work reasonably quickly, booking a job with the Unicorn Theatre for

Children, whose mission it was to inspire children by performing in schools around the country. If one is of a certain age, he might even have seen me. It wasn't exactly rock'n'roll, but it was always inventive, and a lot of fun. It involved travel, camaraderie and doing what I loved most – donning a costume and performing before an audience.

I was also getting paid adequately, if not handsomely, for my work. The only downside was the range of Equity-recommended digs available to us. Equity is the actors' union in the UK, and at that time it was very helpful in recommending housing in the provinces. I can only assume that the people who compiled the list had never actually stayed in any of their recommendations as the accommodation left much to be desired.

In Kings Lynn, our temporary abode comprised the only habitable house in an entire square. Having taken some hits during the war, it was shored up on either side and surrounded by rubble. There was no bathroom and the lavatory was an outhouse in the garden.

'There'll be a jug of water put outside your doors every morning,' the landlady informed us, 'for washing.' Lest we thought we should drink it.

She also warned us that she locked up the house at ten each night. 'What do I do if I want to go to the loo after ten?' I asked politely.

'Your problem,' she replied.

No, your problem, I thought, making a decision then and there that, if necessary, I would simply use the window.

73

Having lived in southern Africa for so long, I was used to taking daily showers, and I was therefore bemused by the British approach to personal hygiene in the 1960s. Inaccessible lavatories, jugs of freezing water in which to wash. Compared to the way of life I had been used to, Britain felt like a step back in time. In Southend, another landlady thought the notion of bathing daily was a tremendous indulgence, and duly charged sixpence for the privilege. Each time I produced my money, on a daily basis, she'd glare as if I was committing a heinous moral crime. Whether she was worried I'd wear out her pristine bathroom or cause the electricity meter to explode from unexpected over-use I don't know, but despite much disgruntled huffing, I got my daily bath.

Towards the end of the tour, the attraction of Equity's recommended B&Bs, was beginning to wear thin, so much so that by the time we got to Ludlow in Shropshire, I went wild. Although our salaries were modest in the extreme, I eschewed the local digs for the comparative luxury of the local inn.

It was heaven. Not least because I was joined in going AWOL by one of my fellow cast members – a girl I had fancied for quite some time. I don't know if it was my charm or the tantalizing thought of staying in a place with running hot water that tempted her, but it was the best night of the entire tour.

Irritating as they were, it wasn't the inconveniences that propelled me back to the African continent; it was the lack of sufficient work. Swinging as it was, there simply weren't enough jobs in London for all of the aspiring actors chasing them. I'd had enough. I was back on a plane to Rhodesia in 1968, heading for the family home in Bulawayo. Despite the constant apprehension over being called up for military service, I thought I would be able to get more of the kind of work I was so keen to do.

Before leaving for Johannesburg in the early 1960s, I had guested regularly on a twice-weekly television entertainment programme. The medium was in its infancy then, and now it was burgeoning. With theatre work drying up, I decided to try and get in on the action.

Ironically, it was in radio that I quickly found love. It, too, was a growing medium in that part of the world, and I soon managed to land regular work. By the early 1970s I'd contributed to every home-produced news programme in Rhodesia, working as a freelancer for the Rhodesia Broadcasting Corporation (RBC).

I stayed six years on that particular visit, but the writing was on the wall. By 1974 the war in Rhodesia had intensified, and we were now expected to do military service on a regular basis by putting in a month's service every six to eight weeks. There was no end in sight, and therefore no future. I was also married by this time, and my wife was expecting our daughter. It was time to take the next sensible step. I had heard that commercial radio – including news radio – had started up in the UK, and with my broadcasting experience, I knew I had a shot at a good job.

I was right. I joined LBC News Radio within a month of our return.

Joining a 24-hour news station was not an easy adjustment. Nonstop airtime requires a significant amount of content and the station needed to be staffed around the clock, which meant working nights. The last time I had worked through the night was during my time in the army either conducting night patrols in the bush or on guard duty at the barracks. I was asked by my station bosses if I would consider doing the overnight news slot. I was a new voice in London broadcasting and prepared to do whatever was necessary to get ahead in a very competitive industry. It wasn't ideal, but I agreed.

Working nights five days a week and then going home to sleep for half the day was not conducive to a happy marriage, and before long I was a single father bringing up my 3½ year old daughter, Victoria.

My immediate priority was to ensure that she had stability and continuity. This meant keeping her in nursery school, though I could ill afford it. I also needed a child minder. Through the small ads in *The Lady* magazine I found an au pair, and the magazine became my bible in the ensuing years.

By this time I was working more sensible hours during the day, and my regular slots included *AM*, LBC's weekend breakfast show. Unfortunately, au pairs didn't work 24/7, which meant that Victoria had to go into work with me at the weekend. LBC was very supportive, and while I entertained Londoners for three hours over their cornflakes, my fellow journalist kept Victoria amused in the newsroom.

Victoria, myself and the au pair were living in a two-bedroomed flat in Windsor, so space was tight. Our first au pair was a wonderful and rather large Austrian lady named Anita. She was a dreadful cook, but redeemed herself by baking the most mouth-watering apple strudel. Victoria adored her. But soon the rented flat gave way to my first mortgage, a three-bedroomed, terraced cottage, also in Windsor. It was a step up for us, but when I got the keys and walked in, I wondered just what I had done and how I was going to cope. There was no carpeting and no furniture, but with the meagre savings I had accumulated, I carpeted the house and bought a fridge, cooker, some chairs and three mattresses. There wasn't enough left over to buy the actual beds.

No matter. I would build some. Having served an apprenticeship for five years, I was good with my hands, and out of necessity knew I could rise to the challenge. I bought wood and screws from a DIY store and built two single beds, a double bed and a rather fine dining table, which started off rectangular, but a couple of years later, I tired of it and adapted it to a round one.

There were still some early morning and late night shifts making transport a problem. I needed a car and knew just where to find one that suited my budget. In the 60s and 70s Australians travelled to Europe in droves. They bought cars, usually Volkswagens, while in Holland, toured the continent and the UK, and when they were done with them, they sold them outside Australia House in London's Aldwych. I wrote off the first one I purchased when I hit black ice and lost control of the car. I thought I was a goner, believing the car would somersault over the wall at the side of the road and onto the railway tracks below, but I survived, and it was back to Australia House to look for another.

The second, another Volkswagen, had a sound enough engine, but the bodywork left much to be desired. In winter there was more ice inside the car than outside, and if I glanced over my shoulder at the floor in the back, I could get a pretty good view of the road. This all took place around the time of the Queen's Silver Jubilee, by which stage my working schedule revolved around outside broadcast events and the royal calendar. These events included the Queen's official birthday parade, Trooping the Colour. As I described the spectacle to the nation, Victoria took in the view from the roof of the news van. She came with me when I commentated at the Remembrance Sunday ceremony in Whitehall; she was alongside me as I broadcast from the Royal Tournament at Earl's Court and she accompanied me to Normandy when I covered the commemorations for the 40th anniversary of D-Day in 1984.

All the while I continued to maintain regular slots on LBC. There was the Christmas Day *AM* breakfast show, during which I'd have Victoria open a Christmas present on-air. One of my guests on the show each year was Savoy chef, Anton Edelmann, who would offer listeners last minute Christmas dinner tips. After the show we would join Anton in his kitchen at the hotel, where he would treat us to a late breakfast of smoked salmon washed down with champagne for me and freshly-squeezed orange juice for Victoria.

Anton was always a kind and generous man. When

it was time to leave, he would thrust a side of smoked salmon into my hands, along with a bottle of his best bubbly. We may have suffered our privations, but our Christmas dinners were always top notch.

Another of my regular LBC slots was the live New Year's Eve broadcast from Trafalgar Square. Victoria was there, too, safe within a secure area set up by the police who acted as her minders while I was on-air.

There's a misconception that if someone is in the entertainment industry he's well off. Nothing could be further from the truth. We lived day to day. I was still driving the car with no floor in the rear. I was still DIY'ing. I was still dependent on au pairs, and still trying to maintain a sense of normality for Victoria, though her young life was not without its challenges. She was never thrilled when work commitments meant I had to drop her off at school an hour before it opened, but just as I was glad to have an understanding bank manager, we were lucky that she had an understanding headmistress.

*

During our pre-visit recce to Hungary we had learned that Budapest was going to present both logistical and security-related challenges. Two walkabouts were scheduled – one in the Central Market Hall, and the other in a nearby square alongside the river Danube. Both locations posed potential threats to the royal couple's safety.

There was particular concern for the Princess. Press speculation was rife with regard to how much weight she had lost. There was no question that she was on the skinny side of slim, but there was also much muttering, especially in the tabloids, about whether she might be suffering from bulimia. I didn't know anything about that, but I had observed that she didn't cope well when she was overly hot or flustered. Any crowd situation – chiefly one in which she had to be dressed formally – had to be monitored carefully.

The Market Hall visit was one in which we could readily see the chance of 'losing it' – press office speak for when the principals are engulfed by a mob of well-wishers. We therefore suggested to the Hungarian security team that they erect barriers along the walkabout route.

The suggestion fell on deaf ears. The security detail looked at us as if we had suggested putting each member of the crowd in chains. 'Barriers keep people *in*,' the lead security officer pronounced, 'and here in Hungary, which is now a democracy, we do not see any need to erect barriers.'

His stern expression made it clear that there was no room for argument.

Fast-forward to the royal visit itself, and exactly what we had predicted came to pass. The royal couple entered the Central Market Hall, and with well-wishers keen to have their moment, we did indeed lose it…and in turn lost them.

No harm was done. We managed to retrieve them just past an array of local cheeses. Having endured minimal trauma via the medium of extreme well-wishing, neither royal visitor appeared to be too traumatized by the experience. Not surprisingly, by the time we reached the next walkabout, in Vidago Square by the river Danube, there were enough barriers in place to adequately contain a thousand fanatical Bolsheviks. After all, no democracy, however proud and new, wants to be responsible for mislaying members of the British Royal Family.

For all the anxiety of the first walkabout, both Charles and Diana worked wonders. This was quite a coup for an eastern bloc country. The local people had never seen royal luminaries at such close quarters, and as they walked, chatted and shook hands one could feel the palpable warmth and affection in the air. Even so, the crowds had taken a toll on the Princess.

'Dickie,' she whispered to me, as we neared the end of the walkabout in Vidago Square. 'I'm feeling terrible. I think I'm going to pass out.'

Though there are plans and protocols in place for countless numbers of potential royal mishaps, there are none for a situation like this. It is generally left to the initiative of whomever is closest at the time. In this case, me.

Her Royal Highness clearly needed to be removed from the site, and quickly. The last thing either of us wanted was for her collapse in the middle of the crowd. Fortunately, the motorcade was parked nearby, in a side road just off the square, which had been sealed off in the event we needed an escape route.

'Just keep walking close beside me,' I told her. 'Keep walking and don't look back. We're nearly there. Take deep breaths…that's it…just keep going.'

I knew where the motorcade was parked; now it was just a case of getting the Princess to it without her keeling over.

Under normal circumstances a person feeling faint is not necessarily a cause for alarm, but these were not normal circumstances. Speculation was ongoing in the newspapers about whether the Princess was struggling with bulimia. I refused to enter into it. All I knew was that to provoke another rush of excitable chit-chat on the subject would benefit no-one, least of all the Princess and her sons.

We made it to the car. Once there, I ensured that she was comfortable. She simply seemed to be suffering from crowd-fatigue. I told the chauffeur – one of ours, who had driven the Prince's Bentley from London – to give her water and to keep an eye on her. I walked back to where the Prince and the Household were saying their goodbyes and briefed the lady-in-waiting as to what had happened, grateful that a small crisis hadn't exploded into a global story.

The following day the Princess was back in fine form, and in a reflective mood. After a display of British fashions at the Museum of Applied Arts in downtown Pest, the Princess was across the river in the old town of Buda. Amongst other magnificent buildings stood the Calvinist Church overlooking the Danube, and the equally magnificent parliament building on the opposite side of the river.

Diana was keen to visit the church, and I had a pretty good idea why. As I had seen her do before, she wanted to slip away from the hustle and bustle for a moment to centre herself through prayer.

I hung back and kept a watchful eye on her from a respectful distance. She went to the front of the nave, fell to her knees and buried her head in her hands. It was an intensely private moment and I lowered my eyes to look away, but not before catching a glimpse of a camera lens poking through a side door.

I crossed the space to collar the surprised photographer, knowing exactly what sort of action to take. Snappers know well how to handle such situations. They keep a spare roll of film handy so that when they're caught taking unsolicited photographs, they hand over a decoy roll.

I was not going to let that happen. 'I want all of it,' I insisted. He didn't try to argue as he knew he'd never see the pictures published without facing a lawsuit. All of his rolls were handed over.

There were no hard feelings. Such is the game between the press and the press office, one in which the score is generally about even.

CHAPTER 7

Breaking News

Cirencester, June 1990

B y the beginning of the 1990s, it was abundantly clear
that all was not well within the Prince and Princess of
Wales's marriage. Nothing had been said on the subject,
and nothing would be. Not by the staff at any rate. As
employees, we were expected to be the souls of discretion.
Loyalty to my employer and her family meant that I
wouldn't enter into gossip about what might or might not
have been going on in their private lives.

There was no doubt that the Prince and Princess's
living arrangements hinted at a marital rift. The Royal
Family has always kept multiple residences, but by now
the Princess was spending all of her time at Kensington
Palace, while Prince Charles was usually to be found at
Highgrove. Whenever possible he would always try to
return to Gloucestershire, even if he had engagements that
required him to be in central London.

With relations as they were, logistics became an even
bigger issue in terms of joint engagements. Charles and

Diana had a full diary of commitments which they were expected to attend together. They would arrive and depart from each engagement as a couple, but what the press didn't know, was that often the royal car would make a stop in Friary Court, St James's Palace, which was in Marlborough Road between the Mall and Pall Mall. There, another car would be waiting to take the Prince to wherever he might be going, while the Princess would continue home to Kensington Palace. It was a necessary performance to avoid giving the circling hacks any indication that trouble was afoot.

I had become accustomed to performing. By the time I began working for the Royal Family, I had experienced many years as both an actor and a broadcaster. Going before the cameras in my new role would have come easily had it not been so frowned upon by the Palace.

That said, one Friday in June 1990, I was left with a difficult choice.

I was at Highgrove with the Prince of Wales, where he was filming a piece for a television documentary marking the 15th anniversary of the Prince's Trust. Charles was a consummate professional in front of the camera, and so the shoot was brief. Once he wrapped, he hurried off to play polo in Cirencester.

Highgrove has a staff dining room just off the kitchen. As soon as the camera crew left I took the opportunity to grab a bite to eat before heading back to London. No sooner had I sat down, then a call came through to let me know that the Prince had taken a tumble and was being driven to nearby Cirencester Cottage Hospital with a suspected broken arm.

Lunch curtailed, I made a run to meet him there. This particular polo match wasn't a major event on the sporting calendar, but both the media and public were always keen to see the Prince play.

With Charles on his way to the hospital, I knew an eager band of journalists wouldn't be far behind. My job was to get there first in order to prevent some poor unsuspecting hospital worker being seized by an overzealous reporter chasing a scoop.

As His Royal Highness was wheeled into theatre – an X-ray having confirmed that his arm was broken in three places above the elbow – the assembled press pack continued to multiply. Armed with what little information had been made available to me, I stepped outside to give a briefing.

The Prince was under anesthetic, and the questions came thick and fast.

'If the arm is broken in three places, will Charles be able to play polo again?'

'If the arm is broken in three places, what are the chances of Charles playing polo again?'

'How will the bones knit together in order that...' – you guessed it – '...the Prince will be able to play polo again?'

The press often asks the same question repeatedly in the hope of tripping up a designated spokesperson. I had already told them the simple facts: yes, the Prince had broken his arm in three places, and yes, he would be able to play polo again. Reporters on the hunt can't help but want for news with more substance. After all, their livelihood depends upon acquiring sufficient copy to fill their editor's bulletins and pages. They persist in squeezing out every last detail from situations which otherwise wouldn't require more than a couple of lines.

With a partially satiated press, I went back inside to call the office with an update.

The Prince returned to his room a couple of hours later, having had the fractures set. I spoke at length to the orthopedic surgeon who had performed the procedure to be absolutely clear on the facts. The afternoon was wearing on, and the crowd out front was becoming restless. Deadlines for the evening news bulletins were rapidly approaching and reporters were desperate for something to put on the air. I made an executive decision, and strode outside once again to give the assembled press a briefing... this time on camera.

It was short and succinct. I explained where and how the arm was broken, detailed the treatment that had been administered and offered assurances that HRH would be back in the saddle again soon.

I returned to pay a final visit to the Prince who was settling in for what his doctors anticipated would be a two-day stay. He had seen my briefing and was gracious enough to thank me for doing as he would have wished without having to ask.

That being my job, I thought nothing more of it. Meanwhile, what was potentially a much bigger news story was unfolding. HRH had a visitor – a Mrs Camilla

Parker Bowles. Where she had sprung from I had no idea, but Charles was clearly pleased to see her. Though he was still woozy from the anesthetic, he was less agitated in her company. She didn't stay long, just long enough to make sure he was comfortable and to assure him that she was close by if needed.

Personally, I never gave her presence much thought. The senior members of the Household knew what was going on, and if the worst came to pass, we would batten down the hatches and ride out the storm.

Over the course of the next two days, I returned to Cirencester to corral the press, and on the morning the Prince was discharged, I was on hand to provide a final briefing.

It had been an eye-opening couple of days. I wasn't privy to Charles and Camilla's meetings, but had I been, and had I ventured an opinion about the potential for exposure, I would have been told in no uncertain terms to get lost.

It was my first real glimpse into the grim reality of the Waleses marital situation. When the Prince left hospital, he and the Princess put on an impressive display of unity, but in reality they were anything but unified.

I had a sense that difficult times lay ahead, but when I finally left for London, my principal feeling was one of profound relief that no-one had cottoned on to the bigger picture. The resultant headlines, particularly in the tabloids, would have been a gift to editors, and the front pages that might have been didn't bear thinking about.

I returned to the Palace feeling rather buoyant. The Prince's arm would heal; the press was satisfied, and best of all there had been no leaks hinting at the much larger fracture – the state of the Waleses marriage. I was surprised, therefore, at the conclusion of the morning meeting when Charles Anson, my senior, asked me to stay behind.

The royal press office then was a very different beast to the one operating today. Where now there is a team of some 27 people, in the late 1980s and early 90s, we were a much smaller affair. There was the press secretary in charge, and three other press secretaries, each with an overall portfolio. John Haslam looked after the Duke of Edinburgh, the Princess Royal and the royal finances. Geoff Crawford looked after Princess Margaret, the Duke and Duchess of York and Prince Edward. I looked after the Prince and Princess of Wales. Five information officers ably backed us up, one of which was responsible for the Court Circular and public enquiries. We were a grand total of nine, and a pretty close-knit team, so I was dismayed to have been singled out to stay after the meeting. I had a feeling that I was about to get a good dressing down. The question was, why?

Charles Anson wasted no time in telling me. My sin proved to be the on-camera briefing I had given outside the hospital. It was not the royal way to speak on camera, and I shouldn't have taken it upon myself to do so. No Buckingham Palace press officer had ever spoken on camera before. Our role was to brief the correspondents off the record, full stop.

I was more than a little irritated. I had done my job professionally, and to the Prince's satisfaction. I was almost 50 years old, and yet I'd been treated like I was new to the game.

I kept my thoughts to myself, but after leaving Anson's office, I put in a call to the Prince of Wales. It was an impulsive act, something I'd never done before, but given that Charles had thanked me personally, I felt that the situation needed to be rectified. In the grand scheme of things it was a minor transgression, especially given the much bigger crisis that had been avoided with reference to Mrs Parker Bowles.

I felt both cheered and vindicated that my little knee-jerk act of petulance paid off. At the morning meeting the following day, Charles Anson explained that HRH had called to say how pleased he was with the way I had handled the broken arm incident.

Despite the call from the Prince, there was no change in Palace policy. The royal communications strategy was stuck in the dark ages, but I toed the line from then on. It would have been nice to set a broadcasting precedent, but I was on staff, and one simply didn't break the rules.

CHAPTER 8

Birthday Boy

September 1990

In 1990 the Princess of Wales threw me a party to celebrate my 50th birthday. There was a drinks reception in her sitting room followed by a sit down lunch in the dining room of the home she shared with Prince Charles at Kensington Palace. I couldn't have been more excited. I've always been a big one for celebrating birthdays. Maybe it has something to do with the emotional challenges of my childhood, but I've always thought birthdays should carry importance. I couldn't give a fig about exchanging Christmas presents, but when it comes to birthdays, I feel quite differently. It's your big day – the one day in the year when you're the centre of attention, and I love the whole idea of making it special.

The Princess was incredibly generous and thoughtful. She loved to surprise people, including those who worked for her. That year I was to be especially spoiled, and my birthday would prove to set a precedent. I wasn't aware of the Princess ever having laid on a party for someone who worked for her. To say I felt privileged would be an understatement.

I was able to invite 20 guests, which gave me the perfect opportunity to share my good fortune with colleagues. I had been at the Palace for two years, and it was thanks to my pretty great workmates that I enjoyed going into the office every day.

The party also gave me the chance to treat a trio of other key women in my life – my second wife Rosemary, my daughter and my mother, who had travelled from Bulawayo in order to celebrate my milestone birthday.

I let Rosemary in on the secret early on, but merely told my mother that we were going out for lunch. Victoria, who was a boarder at Elmhurst Ballet School at the time, was kept completely in the dark.

It had broken my heart to send Victoria to boarding school – not least because it brought back so many of my own painful memories – but having gone as far as she could with an after school ballet teacher, she longed to go to a school dedicated entirely to dance. With classes often going on into the early evening and at weekends, it simply wasn't logical to attend as a day pupil. Although I missed her terribly, she thrived, and as an only child, perhaps she was tailor made for the experience as not only did she relish every minute of her time there, she made wonderful friends for life.

In order to keep up the ruse, it was time to do a little performing myself. I arrived at her school mid-week, which was highly irregular, and told Victoria to change out of her uniform and into her Sunday best as we were going to lunch in London. Dumbfounded to be pulled out of class, she duly did as she was told. I didn't come clean until we turned the car onto Palace Avenue, the private road that leads to Kensington Palace.

'Where are we going,' she asked.

'Oh, didn't I tell you?' I replied. 'The Princess of Wales is giving me a lunch in her apartment, and she invited you too.'

Victoria was speechless, something of a rarity, but her expression was a birthday present in itself. I had already let the cat out of the bag to my mother, as knowing how fastidious she was about her hair, make-up and always wearing the appropriate clothes, I knew she'd be mortified to have not had the opportunity to dress for this one. Telling her was a joy. Considering how much my mother had loved the high life, it was incredibly validating to be in a position to take her to lunch with the wife of the heir to the British throne and future Queen Consort. What's more it was a lunch in her son's honour.

Upon entering apartments eight and nine, Diana's residence until her death, people were immediately struck by how homey it was. While one might expect ornate tapestries, chandeliers and gold leaf ceilings, there was nothing ostentatious about the Princess's house. The address may have read Kensington Palace, but it was a home first and foremost.

When we arrived, we were shown into the drawing room and Diana joined us minutes later. Rendered completely star-struck, my wife, mother and daughter dipped into curtsies. As an avid ballet enthusiast, the Princess broke the ice immediately by telling Victoria that her curtsey was the best. My work duties frequently found me in this same room with Diana, but usually for little more than a quick exchange and a bow. Framed family photographs adorned every surface, and dominating the space was a large grand piano. An accomplished pianist in her own right, I had had the good fortune of hearing Diana play during a tour to Hungary in 1991. As had happened previously in Melbourne in 1988, a brave music professor persuaded her to have a go. Without the aid of sheet music, she skilfully played a section of Rachmaninoff's Concerto Number Two. It was quite something.

A champagne reception ensued, followed by lunch. We entered the dining room, where four tables of five had been set and helium balloons blazing *Nifty Fifty!* graced each of the chairs. Streamers and party poppers also littered the tables, and everyone was in a very festive mood.

Mervyn Wycherley, the Princess's personal chef, prepared a meal that was simple and elegant, but the *pièce de résistance* was my surprise birthday cake. I had gained a reputation among my colleagues for never being without my mobile phone. It was always with me, as I was aptly reminded when the bright blue cake appeared, topped with an enormous sparkler. The cake was fashioned after the iconic Motorola 'brick' mobile of yesteryear and bore the apropos inscription, *You're never alone when Dickie's got his phone!*

It was an extraordinary day and one I will remember always. I was wearing the Hermès tie Diana had given me the year before. On this day she presented me with a bottle-green cashmere jumper from a high-end shop on Jermyn Street. Admittedly, with my deep-rooted notion of keeping things for best, I have never felt an occasion best enough to wear that beautiful sweater. Today it still proudly sits in my wardrobe, as pristine as the day she gave it to me.

It wasn't just my phone that seemed to be permanently welded to my body, but also my favorite suitcase. It was just as well that I wasn't fazed by a nomadic existence, as I was on the road for about a third of my working life. Royal tours might look glamorous, but they aren't an excuse to gad-about on a jolly, rather they are filled with long hours, hectic agendas and protocols that have to be met. They can also be decidedly lonely affairs. In those days every night on the road entailed an evening event of some description, be it state banquets, cocktail receptions or formal meet-and-greets. Having been on parade all day, it wasn't easy to then don formal wear for another evening of monotonous small talk. As soon as they were able, Charles and Diana would bolt to their individual rooms, no doubt craving a little solitude. While they sat on the phone to London, those of us providing the support would change into tracksuits, kick back with a drink and debrief the day. The couple's 1990 tour schedule was no less busy than usual, including visits to Nigeria and Cameroon – two countries I was looking forward to simply due to my fond memories of life in Zimbabwe.

A trip to Africa involved particularly astute planning. The continent didn't have the sophisticated transport infrastructure of the developed world. It was decided that *Britannia*, the royal yacht, would be our base for the tour. The media's internal ground and air transportation was organized in conjunction with the British High Commission based in Lagos, then the capital. The air component for the Prince and Princess, as well as the Household, would employ the Queen's Flight BAe146 aircraft.

The RAF used the January recce for this tour to familiarize itself with the various airports it would use to transport the royal party. It was necessary to do a dry run of the itinerary beforehand, however, as this was Africa and we didn't want to leave anything to chance. With three fuel stops required en route, it took the best part of a day to travel to Lagos from RAF Brize Norton in Oxfordshire. There's no finer way to see the Sahara than from the window of a royal flight. Tamanrasset Airport, deep in the Algerian Sahara, was a memorable stop. I say airport; in reality it was a strip of tarmac and a single modest building that functioned as a terminal, control tower, customs and immigration hall all in one.

It was there that I realized that a royal tour in this part of the world would have more than the usual complement of challenges. The Royal Family was used to roughing it, but the searing heat was oppressive in the extreme. In the coastal cities of Nigeria and Cameroon, we experienced what felt like 100% humidity – even more overbearing than steamy Indonesia. For Sir John Riddell, then Private Secretary, however, one would have thought he had just stepped off the plane and into a balmy British spring garden. I'll never forget the sight of him strolling down the runway, dressed impeccably, as usual, in a crisp shirt and tie beneath a heavy-wool double-breasted suit while the rest of our party staggered around in clothes that looked like they'd been slept in for a week. Sir John was the epitome of an English gentleman – cool as a cucumber, wearing no hat, no sunglasses, not so much as a drop of sun block. Had I a hat, I would have raised it to him.

The Nigerian tour took in Lagos, Port Harcourt, Maiduguri and Enugu. It was in Maiduguri that the Princess, this time accompanied by the Prince, paid a visit to a leprosy hospital with a call-in to the Molai Centre. Once again she debunked the 'do not touch' myth, informing reporters that leprosy wasn't contagious, and that victims of the ailment shouldn't be shunned. Maiduguri is in the north-east corner of Nigeria, near the border with Chad, and on our last day in the country Charles and Diana were treated to a Durbar – a celebration in their honour. We had been told during the recce that the event would last half an hour. More than an hour after the ceremony had begun, Their Royal Highnesses were still sitting alongside the region's ruler (Nigeria is a Federation of States, each with a ruler or governor) as waves of tribespeople on foot and on horseback made their way across what can only be described as a dust bowl the size of a football field. Also on display was a large number of ululating women, whose unmistakable greeting call – a high, yodel-like trill – is heard in many parts of the African continent.

The procession felt like it would never end, to the point that one member of the media pack quipped that perhaps the parade was running a circular route. For their part Charles and Diana displayed true British stoicism, as the long journey and late hour had no doubt taken a toll before the celebration had even started. The royal couple finally departed with scores of gifts and a fine layer of reddish dust covering them from head to toe. A quick look around confirmed that we were indeed all caked with it, except of course for Sir John Riddell.

At last it was back on to the Queen's plane for the return flight to *Britannia*, via Enugu in eastern Nigeria. The yacht would then sail the short distance to the port of Douala, Cameroon's largest city. I on the other hand, along with my assistant, Kiloran McGrigor and the Princess's policeman, Ken Wharfe, travelled on the press plane to Cameroon's capital Yaoundé, where we would kill 36 hours.

With the plane locked and loaded, and a knackered press corps comatose in its seats, we kicked back ready to relax for the duration of the flight. It was then that the captain suddenly exited the cockpit, opened the outside door and jumped down on to the tarmac. Concerned, I unbuckled my seatbelt and followed him down the steps, which had hastily been put in place. A decidedly incongruous site greeted me. A fire truck had been parked right up against the nose of the plane, preventing us from moving.

'Money,' the captain explained. 'The airport manager says the aircraft's fuel, taxes and landing fees haven't been paid.'

'That's nonsense,' I exclaimed.

Not only had they been paid in full, but the High

Commission had acted as a guarantor for all payments due. This was clearly a case of creative accounting. The ever-resourceful airport manager thought he'd make a bit of extra cash on the side. Diplomatic relations were breaking down at a rapid pace. I stepped in and told the manager I had an armed policeman on board who was tired, covered in dust and in a very bad mood.

'Do you want me to call him off the plane?' I asked.

The bluff worked. After much huffing and puffing, the fire truck was duly moved, and we took off without further incident, headed for the Cameroonian capital of Yaoundé.

Once in Yaoundé, as the press settled into its hotel, the three of us in the advance party planned to make the most of the time we had to kill before the Prince and Princess arrived.

Someone, certainly not me, suggested we play a round of golf. Outnumbered by Kiloran and Wharfie, I had no choice but to agree. Using borrowed clubs from the hotel, we trotted off to play a round on the adjacent course. My golf prowess being distinctly limited, I did the best I could. Thankfully, the round was to be short lived.

'Is that a snake?' asked Ken, casually, as we approached one of the greens. He pointed to an unusual black shape in the grass.

With a single nod I confirmed that it was. From my time in the Rhodesian army, I knew immediately that it was a black mamba, the deadliest snake on the African continent.

Eyebrows shot up.

99

'...And where there is one,' I added, 'there will almost certainly be another.'

Our round ended there, with a hasty sprint off the fairway. Golf being one of my least favourite pastimes, I was quite happy to hightail it to the bar instead.

Our final stop in Cameroon entailed the Prince's visit to Limbe Botanic Gardens, remembered not only for their beauty, but for how desperate I was to get out of there. I don't recall ever experiencing such dizzying heat, particularly as we entered an amphitheatre to watch a group of local singers and dancers. It felt as if we'd entered a sauna from which there was no escape. The Prince coped remarkably well, no surprise as he takes after his parents who have an astonishing capacity for tolerating discomfort when in public. That said, I'm sure we were all eager to return to the cool comfort of the royal yacht back in Douala.

There would be a quick turnaround as a black tie reception was to be held on board that evening. I showered and changed in about ten minutes, but fate was not on our side that day. The Admiral informed us that jellyfish had been sucked into the system while en route from Lagos, disabling the air conditioning – at last, something that did cause Sir John to break a sweat.

CHAPTER 9

Heir Raising

December 1992

During my time at the Palace I didn't see a great deal of Princes William and Harry. Always in the limelight, Diana was well aware of the emotional toll royal life could take, and as a result she was eager to protect her children from the media glare for as long as possible. She took great pains to separate her role as a mother from her role as the wife of the heir to the throne. In doing so she hoped to provide the boys with as normal a childhood as one could have within the confines of Palace walls. She took them to movies, theme parks and burger restaurants, each activity allowing for the boys to have a life in common with their friends. She rarely brought them into the office at St James's Palace. Unless there was a photo call at Ludgrove, their prep school, I seldom had the opportunity to spend time with them, but there is one occasion in particular that sticks out in my mind.

In December 1992, the Princess held a pre-Christmas drinks reception at Kensington Palace to thank her charities for their work over the course of the year. At the time Diana was president or patron of over 100 organizations including Barnardo's, Centrepoint, Great Ormond Street Children's Hospital, the Leprosy Mission, the National AIDS Trust, the Royal Marsden Hospital NHS Trust and Help the Aged, to name but a few. She knew how much her involvement meant in terms of monies raised, and she didn't just serve as a pretty figurehead; she worked tirelessly to help disadvantaged people across all demographics.

An ardent music lover, she liked nothing more than to attend a concert. Verdi's 'Requiem' was her favorite piece of classical music, but she also enjoyed pop and rock. Such evenings out didn't just provide welcome downtime, they also opened up her social circle to a world of celebrity friends.

It was easy to be intimidated within the environs of a palace, especially when in the presence of royalty. Diana knew there was nothing like a sprinkling of pop stars to make such a reception go with a swing.

My wife and daughter had also been invited. Victoria was still collecting herself from having just entered five steps behind Elton John, when Diana made a beeline toward us saying, 'Victoria, have you met George Michael?'

My daughter, then 18, replied with a wide-eyed, 'no…'

Diana leaned in and whispered, 'Isn't it a shame he doesn't like the ladies?'

We hadn't realized that a rather mischievous eight-year-old Prince Harry was standing right next to her until he tugged on her skirt and asked in a loud voice, 'Who doesn't like the ladies, Mummy?'

Mortified, Diana exclaimed in a loud whisper, 'Shut up, Harry!' She went on to say to him, 'Why don't you take your friend Victoria to meet George Michael?'

'Who's my friend Victoria?' Harry wanted to know.

The Princess pointed to my still-gobsmacked daughter. 'This is your friend Victoria...now off you go.'

They scurried away, and I neither saw nor heard anything from Victoria until the reception was over. During the short walk home she was like a broken record. 'George Michael said this, George Michael said that!'

George Michael, as it happened, had said rather a lot...much to her delight.

I, however, was impressed with another young man that night – one that would go on to have a George of his own. The Princess was always well aware of William's destiny, and began teaching him the ways of kingship from a very early age. Part of that learning included the art of public speaking. To everyone's delight, as the evening came to a close a ten-year-old Prince William stood to make his first speech. It was a simple statement thanking the staff on behalf of his mother for all their help and support over the past year, but it also represented a major milestone in his young royal life. His mother, so incredibly proud, stood beaming as she hung on his every word.

October 1991 saw Charles and Diana head off for a royal tour to Canada, and I was thrilled when I learned that our base would once again be the royal yacht *Britannia*. She served as a home-from-home floating palace. By Royal Navy standards she was elegant, comfortable and functional, but by no means luxurious. In fact compared to the multi-million pound super yachts that line the harbours of Saint-Tropez today, she was positively modest. The Queen has never been one for ostentation.

There are two rooms for entertaining – the Royal Dining Room and the Drawing Room and Ante Room, the former decorated with gifts given to the Queen during her numerous visits abroad. There's a 1738 broadsword presented by the Swedish Navy in 1956, a Narwhal's tusk presented by former Canadian Prime Minister, Pierre Trudeau, in 1970, and a seven-foot rib bone from a whale found by the Duke of Edinburgh on Deception Island in the South Shetlands, in 1957.

The large mahogany and ebony table, specifically made for the yacht, is the centerpiece of the Royal Dining Room. In the alcoves are smaller tables, two of which came from the second HMY *Victoria and Albert* (1855 to 1900). These could be added to the larger table to form a 'U' formation, which is usually how it was set up for official or state meals.

The Drawing Room and Ante Room were combined, forming a useful, cosy and unpretentious space. The rooms were furnished with gifts from the Swedish Royal Family in 1956. Additional pieces came from the third royal yacht to be called *Victoria and Albert* (1901 to 1937).

The drawing room was also home to a couple of unique treasures – a baby grand piano said to have once been played by Noël Coward and a tattered white ensign that had flown from Captain Scott's sledge during his last ill-fated expedition to Antarctica. History doesn't come more moving than that.

Along with the equerry and protection officer, I had been on the ground for two days prior to the Prince and Princess. On the eve of their arrival, FORY (Flag Officer Royal Yacht – effectively the captain) held a dinner for the assembled group. FORY, Rear Admiral Bob Woodard, was a man with the warmest and most incredible sense of humour. In his inimitable way he kept us wildly entertained throughout the meal. He turned over the floor on occasion, and this particular night he asked each of us what our favorite food was.

Not being a foodie, I was a little stumped until I remembered how I used to breakfast on Christmas Day in the old days back in Rhodesia. As Christmas fell mid-summer, breakfast was taken outside by the pool. My festive menu consisted of a whole grapefruit, followed by kippers and toast, all washed down with champagne.

'Champagne in Rhodesia?' Bob said, stunned. 'Good God! Sounds like the high-life. Weren't they under sanctions back then?'

'Yes,' I confirmed. 'Indeed they were.'

We even had a royal navy frigate patrolling the waters outside the Port of Beira just in case anyone peddling sanctioned goods managed to find a way in. It made not the slightest difference. We never seemed to run short of life's little luxuries, including champagne at Christmas.

We retired to the drawing room for a nightcap and I thought nothing more of it.

The next day would be a busy one, preparing for the arrival of the Prince and Princess, followed by a jam-packed schedule for the ensuing six days. With that in mind, I toddled off to bed and awoke the next morning eager to begin.

Breakfast was served in the Royal Dining Room, and as I approached I was hit by an aroma that took me back a good 25 years. Alongside the usual cereals, bacon and sausages were grapefruit and kippers. Placed on a side table nearby was an ice bucket containing a bottle of champagne.

It took all of two seconds to calculate that with the royal flight not arriving until teatime, we could all indulge in a glass of bubbly as we sat down to savour an unforgettable breakfast. Bob did us proud.

Half term saw the arrival of Princes William and Harry, along with their nanny, Jessie Webb. Their arrival 36 hours before their parents brought with it everything you'd expect when two young boys, aged nine and seven respectively, find themselves corralled in a relatively confined space. Their laughter, energy and contagious lust for life reverberated throughout the yacht. It was my first occasion witnessing the family together in such close quarters, and I was struck by the close bond that both parents had with their children.

The Princes had clearly enjoyed their time in Canada with their nanny, but it was obvious how much they were looking forward to seeing their mum and dad. They lined up on deck ready for their parents' appearance at the port, offering the occasional wave to well-wishers crowding the dock. We could all feel their barely-contained excitement and sense of anticipation. The Princess, eager to see her sons, was the first out of the car. Acknowledging a salute from the Officer of the Watch and a bow from the Admiral, she rushed with outstretched arms towards William and hugged him tightly. The Prince, who had been in Scotland before joining the Princess for the flight to Canada, hadn't seen his sons in a month and was equally keen to see the boys. He held Harry close before parents and children swapped, and the family retired arm-in-arm into the yacht.

For a relatively ordinary event – parents greeting their children – it made for a particularly moving moment. The demands of royal life often require parents to be separated from their children for long stretches of time, which makes reunions that much more poignant.

But the media tends to have a hard heart. The photos that flashed around the world only told half the story. There was no picture of Charles hugging William or Harry, just one of the Princess greeting William, arms wide open. The press was actively speculating about the state of the royal marriage, but to deliberately distort what was clearly a family affair was to my mind very sad. Whatever the accusations lobbed at the Prince – and there were many – to insinuate by omission that he was a less than devoted father felt very unjust.

This had, however, become par for the course, and we knew there was only more to come.

CHAPTER 10

A Picture Tells a Thousand Words

February 1992

Prince Charles had visited India as a single man of 32 in 1980. Sitting on a stone bench beneath the Taj Mahal, the iconic symbol of love, he had vowed to return one day with the woman he loved. Twelve years later his comments were uppermost in our minds as we began to plan for the Prince and Princess of Wales's joint tour to the country. The ripples of concern about their marriage had escalated into much bigger waves, and I was beginning to suspect the worst. All marriages go through bad patches, but I knew this union well and was aware that the cracks were probably getting too great to be papered over.

I didn't cover Prince Charles's solo visit to India, but everyone knew that the stone bench in front of the Taj Mahal was the customary place for VIPs to be photographed when visiting the monument. Arguably India's most well-known and revered tourist attraction, the white marble mausoleum was one of the must-sees that the

Indian authorities insisted on incorporating into any high profile tour.

Mughal Emperor Shah Jahan built the temple to serve as a private mausoleum in memory of his beloved third wife, Mumtaz Mahal, who had died bearing his 14th son. Given the monument's sacred status as a tomb, the rules were very clear – no photography either on or directly in front of the memorial. The bench therefore was the favoured alternative photo spot, and it was by far the best place to appreciate the incredible beauty of one of the great wonders of the world.

The tour had already presented those of us in charge of planning it an almighty headache, particularly with regard to the media. The first Gulf war had delayed the trip by a year, allowing for marital relations to decline even further. Here was a couple in the midst of a private personal war, and yet they were going to have to be with each other around the clock for a week under the relentless glare of the press. It wasn't going to be easy for anybody, and the likelihood of a romantic photo-op of the couple seated before such a grand tribute to love was looking increasingly slim.

I was particularly concerned about Diana. She wasn't good in hot, humid environments. We had to plan her engagements carefully, and ensure that an air-conditioned car was on hand to provide an escape from the heat and crowds whenever necessary. More worrying, however, was that she was obviously in a great deal of emotional pain, and I feared for her stamina.

The first day of any official tour is invariably the hardest, as it tends to involve many rigid, formal protocols.

Each country has a set programme, which usually kicks off with a ceremonial arrival, with the emphasis very much on the word 'ceremony'. There are dozens of hands to be shaken, a head of state, government representative or a slew of dignitaries to meet, and a degree of solemnity is required when paying respects to whichever national or state memorial is being honoured.

Following the day's extensive activities, there will almost certainly be a state banquet in the evening – more hands to shake, more polite chit-chat, more speeches. It all makes for a trying test of endurance.

India was to be no different. After the flight from London to Delhi, the royal couple hit the ground running. There was no time to relax and recover from the journey. They were royals, and royals got on with the job at hand. They had no choice.

In the heat of the unforgiving afternoon sun, the couple arrived at the presidential residence on the first day. Specially invited guests had been waiting for at least an hour under the shade of a canvas awning, while the guard of honour had formed to await inspection under the harsh sunlight.

The ground had been repeatedly watered in an effort to keep the dust levels down, but the authorities were fighting a losing battle. No sooner had the water hit the ground than it dried almost instantaneously. For those of us present, a fine layer of dust covered our skin and clogged our throats.

Rashtrapati Bhavan, the 340-roomed Presidential Palace, is the largest residence of any head of state in the world. It is where the Prince's beloved great-uncle Lord Louis Mountbatten, the last Viceroy of India, resided in 1947 during the twilight years of the British Empire. Forty-five years later, the Prince and Princess of Wales were to be guests of President Venkataraman, in the same Palace once known as Viceroy's House.

One of the charming aspects of official visits is that quite often the hosts themselves will escort the guests to their suite. And so it was that with the formalities over, the President escorted the Prince and Princess to their quarters. With barely an hour to freshen up, they were then promptly whisked away to Raj Ghat, one of India's holiest sites.

Raj Ghat is the black-marbled memorial platform to the father of India, Mahatma Gandhi, and marks the sacred spot where he was cremated in 1948. In a brief but solemn ceremony, the Prince paid tribute to Gandhi by laying a floral wreath. He then returned to the Palace for a meeting with the President, followed that evening by a reception in the Palace gardens.

Aided by a favourable five-and-a-half hour time difference, the Prince and Princess were not as yet showing any signs of fatigue.

Two royals in the mix makes the planning of tour programmes particularly tricky, especially when a large area of ground needs to be covered. In the case of the Prince and Princess, the biggest media draw at the time, there was only one way achieve all that was required diplo-matically – give them separate itineraries. This caused disappointment in some quarters and required a spot of creative thinking, not least in the matter of the trip to the Taj Mahal.

The idea of the Prince and Princess going to the Taj Mahal together had been discussed at length during the recce. A joint visit would have given the world's media the money shot. And yet, we had Diana scheduled to be in Agra, while at the same time Charles was committed to a conference (related to his International Business Leaders Forum) 1,200 miles away in Bangalore, where he was due to give the only keynote address of the tour. A conundrum in the extreme. Charles, who had once vowed that, 'One day I would like to bring my bride here,' was not going to be where we needed him most – seated next to his wife on a bench in front of the bloody Taj Mahal!

A rumbling of media interest could be heard the minute the schedule was made public. Before Their Royal Highnesses had even stepped foot on the plane, newspaper headlines screamed, *Di To Visit Taj Mahal On Her Own*.

Invitations had already gone out for the conference in Bangalore, and we had received acceptance from both British and Indian delegates across the board. Accounting for travel time between cities and his commitment to the forum, His Royal Highness had no interest in changing the arrangements. We were left with no alternative but to bite the bullet.

I was told not to broach the subject further with the Prince, and the programme was set in place. Perhaps he simply felt that it would have been hypocritical to go, and no doubt he was tired of the whole charade. Under the circumstances it would have been excruciating for them both. They no longer had the will to care.

Public reaction was as expected. The media had a field day. Indeed, tabloid editors had struck gold. Considering the manipulative nature of the images of Diana, a lone figure on that infamous bench, it was almost too easy to write the accompanying captions:

Wistful.

Temple of loneliness.

Symbol of a failed marriage.

The list goes on. Gleefully they littered the front pages with their commentary on the significance of the Princess's solo visit, which ironically took place just three days before Valentine's Day.

Based in Bangalore, where I was supporting the Prince at his business meeting, I could only observe the events in Agra with mounting gloom. Our worst fears were being realised several hundred miles away. Sky News reporter Simon McCoy asked the Princess what she had thought of the magnificent tomb. She paused for a few seconds, choosing her words carefully, and then fired her first public shot across the Prince's bow.

'It was a healing experience…very healing.'

Keen for her to elaborate, McCoy asked, 'What do you mean exactly?'

It was a question that would reward him well. After another pause, the Princess replied with a gleam in her eye, 'work it out for yourself.'

I could imagine the delight with which he greeted

those words. Not only did the press pack have their pictures, they now had their story to go with them.

In saying what she did, Diana had effectively given the media carte blanche to write whatever they damn well pleased. A resolute silence would have been the less inflammatory choice, but I appreciated that her frustration had been pushed to the limit, and I couldn't help but sympathize with her. The Prince could have used the visit to the Taj Mahal to make a positive statement about his marriage, and in turn quell the ever-present rumours. Instead his unwavering refusal to accompany her made it clear to both his wife and the world at large that he no longer cared what people thought.

Later, he did publicly admit that he had got it wrong, claiming that some people might have thought him a fool for not joining her. 'A wiser man,' he reflected, 'probably would have done so.' But truth be told he was never going to change his mind however robustly we tried to make him. It would have been a sham, and I think he decided that whatever the repercussions, he was no longer prepared to play the game.

If the media thought the debacle at the Taj Mahal would prove to be the scoop of the century, they hadn't banked on the gift they were about to receive on the eve of Valentine's Day. The royal party had been geographically reunited in the ancient city of Jaipur, the magnificent capital of Rajasthan, which had been painted pink to create a festive air in honour of a visit by Queen Victoria's husband, Prince Albert, in 1853.

The Prince was asked to play in an exhibition polo match and, buoyed by the invitation after so much angst and negative press, he was visibly looking forward to it.

The same could not be said for Diana. An exhibition match requires an official prize giving at its conclusion. It was understood that the Princess would present the prizes, and it was also assumed that win or lose, she would kiss her husband. The Princess, however, was in no mood to be an accessory to the day's events.

During a break for lunch, word came through that the Princess had no intention of attending the polo. The tour's private secretary Peter Westmacott and I went to see her in an effort to persuade her of the wisdom of doing otherwise.

'I don't want to go,' she argued. 'And I have no intention of doing so.'

Her steely expression told us she wasn't going to budge. This left Peter and me metaphorically rolling up our sleeves; we had a job on our hands – Diana simply had to attend the polo.

We were a two-pronged offensive.

'Ma'am, think how it'll look,' we began. 'Think how it'll seem to our hosts and the Indian people. Think how it'll make you look, and how the press will respond. If you fail to show up, you'll be playing right into their hands. Speculation will be rampant.'

We did not receive the desired response. 'You think I even care?' she raged. 'You *really* think I even care anymore? Because I don't! I'm at the point where I don't care what they think, much less what they write in the papers. I'm not going to present the prizes and that's that!'

But that couldn't be that. Were she to skip the prize giving, she would not only be offending her Indian hosts but the Indian people as a whole. As we tried to coax her into changing her mind, we heard that tens of thousands of spectators were pouring into the grounds to watch the match.

We were forced to step it up a notch. The Prince aside, there were two teams of players eagerly anticipating the opportunity to play for her, and who deserved the privilege of shaking her hand at the end of the match. This was the royal tour ethos.

We changed tack again, restating how the snub to the Indian people would be perceived.

Not to be forgotten, the next stop on the Princess's itinerary was Mother Teresa's Mission in Calcutta. The last thing Diana needed if she persisted in her refusal to go to the polo was to know that she had upset her gracious hosts.

It was a game of one-upmanship, and I felt sorry for her. Was the presentation of these prizes really so important as to cause so much distress? Of course not. But we practiced the emotional blackmail anyway because in the clear light of day, making the right professional choice mattered to Diana…which is why she finally agreed to go.

The venue for the match, the Rajasthan Polo Club, was an opulent, flamboyant setting. Smartly dressed in blue double-breasted blazers accessorized with silk cravats, officers of the

Me and my dad in the summer of 1946, months before he died.

Not quite Denis Compton – he gave me the cricket bat. My
mother is the glamorous wicket keeper, *c.* 1948.

Chilling out with the snappers in Nigeria.

Celebrating my 50th Birthday lunch at Kensington Palace, given by
the Princess of Wales. Diana took the picture.

The Prince of Wales' polo fall in Cirencester, June 1990.

I brief the press following the accident.

Press Association's Ron Bell and I chat with Princess Diana at the
Metropolitan Police training college in Hendon, north London.

On duty with the Princess during the summer of 1988.

I accompany Prince Charles on a visit of Hong Kong in November 1992.

The day a nation mourned (*from left to right*): Prince Philip, Prince William, Earl Spencer, Prince Harry and Prince Charles walk behind the King's Troop Royal Horse Artillery at the funeral of Princess Diana in 1997.

Compering a charity Christmas show at Queens Ice & Bowl.

Royal Commentators father and daughter outside Kensington
Palace. During the 2011 Royal Wedding Victoria was with CBS
and I was with Sky News.

61st Cavalry mingled around the clubhouse in a place where it seemed that time had stood still. It was as though we had been transported back to the days of the Raj.

Regimental grooms in jodhpurs, puttees and stiffened turbans emulating those of their officers added to the magnificence, and amidst the vibrancy was the Prince's host, the titular Maharaja of Jaipur, or as he was affectionately known, 'Bubbles Jaipur'.

The Maharaja's English nanny had bestowed the nickname upon him in 1931. She'd been so taken aback by the amount of champagne flowing at the celebration of his birth that she had coined the name Bubbles, which stuck with him until his death in 2011.

The polo event was an important part of the tour, and to the delight of the media in attendance, it was quite a photogenic one as well. Security-wise it was a nightmare, with a crowd exceeding 30,000, but everything went according to plan without incident.

The Prince scored three of his team's four goals, sealing their victory, which seemed to please everyone present, bar one. As the crowd surged onto the pitch, my gaze moved to the royal enclosure, now sealed off with rope. It was impossible to hear anything over the din of the spectators as the teams lined up for the prize giving.

Prince Charles's expression said it all. His face was flushed with the glow of victory, a fine feat for someone who had only recently suffered a nasty fracture, and who was the first to admit to his relative lack of prowess at the sport of kings.

In contrast, the Princess looked as though she'd rather be anywhere else. Perhaps it was Diana's transparent body language that caused the Prince to commit the ultimate faux pas. Instead of leaning in for the requisite kiss after receiving his prize, he turned and walked away. Realising his mistake he hastily returned and, with an uncertain crowd looking on, moved to kiss his wife's right cheek. Incensed, the Princess swiveled her head so that the kiss landed near her ear.

The crowd, as well as those of us accompanying the royal couple, could only cringe. The Prince had clearly been intentionally humiliated, and we knew he'd be furious.

More importantly from our point of view, the Princess had given the press a picture that said it all.

When Ken Wharfe, the Princess's protection officer, later asked Diana why she had behaved as she did, she replied, 'I'm not about to pander to him! Why the bloody hell should I? If he wants to make a fool out of me with that woman, he deserves it. But I am *not* about to make a fool of myself so that all his friends can laugh at me.'

I could understand her reasoning, but that was not how the Prince and his staff saw it.

'She is nothing but a spoilt schoolgirl,' one of his household told me. He went on to accuse her of calculated, childish petulance.

I defended her position – the only one, it would seem, willing to do so – but my argument fell on deaf ears. The Prince's aide simply shrugged his shoulders.

'Surely she could put on a show just once,' he said, before turning his back.

As I watched him skulk off, it occurred to me that that is what Diana had been doing for most of her adult life. I wondered if she was not due some time off for good behavior…time to just be herself.

Whatever arguments and denials I might have made, the pictures published on Valentine's Day spoke volumes.

The royal couple parted company again soon after – the Prince off to Nepal and the Princess headed for a visit to the Mother Teresa Mission in Calcutta.

Meanwhile, those of us in the press office were left to handle damage control.

CHAPTER 11

The *Annus Horribilis* Begins

January 1992

When it comes time to write the history of Queen Elizabeth II's reign, historians, royal commentators and armchair watchers alike will probably agree that 1992 was the worst year in the history of the modern British Monarchy. It even stands to eclipse the abdication crisis of 1936, in which the Queen's uncle, Edward VIII, stepped down claiming memorably that he wasn't prepared to become King, 'without the help and support of the woman I love.'

As usual, the year began with the Queen in residence at Sandringham, quietly marking the anniversary of her accession. The troubles started soon after, with Charles and Diana's ill-fated trip to India. Behaving as they had, the sovereign's immediate family members were directly responsible for a run of negative press aimed at tearing the Windsors to pieces. While the Monarch couldn't be held personally accountable for the Waleses actions, anti-monarchists were quick to lay the blame squarely at her feet. Opinion polls at the year's end didn't quite indicate the demise of the Royal Family, but they did show that the institution of the Monarchy had suffered a significant blow.

Where the Queen was concerned, it was business as usual. We in the press office anticipated another fairly routine year in which Her Majesty would undertake her constitutional and representational duties as head of state and – in her less formal role as Head of the Nation – continue to act as a focus of national identity and pride.

But neither the Queen nor her staff lived in a bubble. By the time the Prince and Princess of Wales returned from India, public and press speculation about their marriage was in overdrive. Indeed with heavy newspaper coverage of the Waleses troubles, as well as speculation of Prince Andrew's marriage to Sarah Ferguson and the divorce of Princess Anne and Captain Mark Phillips, the Royal Family seemed to have a monopoly on column inches.

Predictably, Diana quickly redeemed herself in the eyes of the media. Though unable to meet Mother Teresa (who'd been detained in Rome after suffering a mild heart attack), she'd finished the India tour by singing with other nuns in the Mission chapel and visiting a home for abandoned children. Both events had moved the Princess – and even a few of the more cynical members of the media pack – to tears.

She went on to visit a hospice, and with the distress she experienced there splashed across the world's newspapers, a shift in perception immediately became evident. Reportedly cast aside by her husband and missing her sons, who were halfway across the world, one couldn't help but sympathize with her circumstances. It was no wonder that she came across as rather fragile, and it was good for her to leave the country as soon as possible, if only to keep busy and escape the relentless speculation.

She flew first to Rome to meet the convalescing Mother Teresa, and then in May she headed off for a 36-hour stay in Budapest.

The purpose of the short trip was to raise the profile of the Peto Institute for Conductive Education, an organization with which Diana had links through one of her UK charities. Its mission is to help children suffering from neural disabilities such as cerebral palsy.

Though brief, the visit still needed to be recced. Along with a protection officer, I flew to Budapest beforehand to make a dry run and check the accommodation – in this case the British Ambassador's residence, where a reception was to be held. As patron of the English National Ballet, Diana would also attend the company's gala performance at Budapest's Opera House.

On the morning prior to her arrival, I held my usual press briefing, going over the itinerary and detailing the logistics of time, travel and the various facilities that would be made available. As I spoke, it seemed as though the assembled journalists were much more preoccupied with another matter. A hand shot up before I'd even finished asking for questions.

'This book...what do you know about it?'

'What book?' I responded, having no idea what he was talking about.

'Andrew Morton's kiss-and-tell about Charles and Diana's marriage. Is there any truth to the rumour that she's collaborating with him?'

This was news to me...potentially explosive news. I knew Andrew Morton's name; he was a well-known former tabloid journalist. Could it be true? Given the unusually large and enthusiastic press presence in the room, I couldn't help but think that it was. They certainly weren't there to hear about cerebral palsy.

'I know nothing about it,' I told them truthfully.

'But what do you think? Apparently it's going to be quite explicit.'

Not willing to join in the speculation, I told them only that I would get back to them after I had spoken with the Princess.

With a story as catastrophic as this stood to be, it was essential to be in full possession of the facts. We in the press office could not afford to be reactive. On the contrary, it was imperative that we retained some control in the handling of an issue that would no doubt dominate the headlines.

Had Diana actually co-operated with Morton? Would she really have done such a thing? I needed to find out for myself.

During the visit to the Peto Institute, I managed to steal a private moment with the Princess away from the assembled crowd. I told her about the reporters' questions, emphasizing what seemed to be the widely held belief that she had co-operated with Andrew Morton during the writing of the book.

'What shall I tell them, Ma'am?'

At first she seemed dismayed. Then her expression changed to one of defiance. She fixed me with a stern glare.

'What book? Dickie, I am not collaborating on any book. I know as much about it as they do,' she said, indicating the awaiting press with a nod.

'Okay, Ma'am,' I replied. 'Then that's what I shall tell them.'

'Good!'

My gut feeling was that she was being economical with the truth, but I wasn't about to accuse her of lying. Instead I did as promised and relayed to the media our conversation, offering not a hint of my own thoughts on the matter.

I'm quite sure no-one believed me.

As I expected, Diana continued the charade for months as the year's schedule of events and trips continued as planned. No sooner would she return to London from a trip than she was off again. En route to Diana's solo visit to Egypt, the Queen's Flight BAe 146 actually made a stop to drop off her husband in Turkey, where he was going on a holiday without the Princess. Charles's act was emblematic of the level of discord within the Waleses marriage.

The couple were later reunited on May 21st, as the Princess was scheduled to accompany Charles at the opening of the British Pavilion at Expo '92 in Seville. It was painfully obvious that the couple didn't want to be in each other's company. At every photo opportunity they went to such extreme lengths as to stand apart and cast their gazes outward – anything to avoid eye contact.

It was painful to witness, and I'm sure I wasn't the only one watching the relationship unravel who wished that it could just be done with.

Soon it would all come to a head anyway. It was upon their return from Seville that the much-anticipated bombshell finally detonated...when Andrew Morton's forthcoming book, *Diana: Her True Story*, was serialized in *The Sunday Times*.

The Princess had succeeded brilliantly in covering up the fact that she had indeed collaborated with Morton. She had even kept the secret from some who were prepared to speak on her behalf, including her brother-in-law, Sir Robert Fellowes, the Queen's private secretary at the time.

Also left in the dark was Lord McGregor, then chairman of the Press Complaints Commission who, following the initial serialization in the paper, publically rushed to her defence, lambasting the *The Sunday Times* for, 'dabbling their fingers in the stuff of other people's souls.'

We received word of the serialization on Saturday, the eve of its publication. Knowing that *The Sunday Times* had a two week exclusive, we were sure that the paper would milk the story for all it was worth. Late that night, I made a trip from Windsor to London's Charing Cross Station in order to pick up first copies, hot off the presses.

I braced myself for what I was about to read.

The next morning the first call I received was not from a member of the press, but from the Princess herself. I assumed that she, too, had sent out the night before for a first edition, and though she didn't say so, I suspected that she'd passed a sleepless night reading and re-reading the extract.

'What do I do, Dickie?' There was an edge of panic in her voice. 'What do I do?'

'There's nothing you can do, Ma'am,' I replied, curtly. 'You've let the cat out of the bag. It's done.'

'Yes, but what should I *do*?' she repeated.

'All you can do, Ma'am, is batten down the hatches. Don't talk to anyone...and I mean anyone. And while you're at it,' I added, hoping to lighten the moment, 'why don't you pour yourself a large scotch and get drunk?'

'Mmm,' she said, distracted. 'I might just have to do that. I'll call you later, okay?'

I didn't hear from her again that day.

In fact I took no more than a dozen calls, mostly from reporters obligated to ask for a response from the Palace and knowing full well all they would receive was 'if you've read the serialization, you must draw your own conclusion.' Besides, they had much more interesting meat to pull apart – the contents of *Diana: Her True Story*.

The book became a runaway bestseller, and the Princess could do nothing but keep her head down. She continued to maintain the line that she had had nothing to do with the writing of it. I had my doubts, but it was entirely her prerogative.

As the year went on, there was no respite from the

relentlessly salacious, and often negative, press directed towards the Royal Family. In August, pictures emerged of financial advisor John Bryan sucking the toes of a topless Duchess of York while the two were on holiday in the south of France. Taken at a private villa, the pictures indicated a blatant invasion of privacy.

Sarah happened to be at Balmoral with the rest of the Royal Family at the time that the photos were splashed across the British Sunday tabloids. The publication did not go down well. The Queen's private secretary suggested that the Duchess might feel better if she left the rest of the family and returned immediately to London. Never one for giving much credence to the suggestions of private secretaries, on this occasion, Sarah heeded the advice.

It was *The Mirror* that had initially broken the story, making the most of their scoop by publishing ten pages of scandalous pictures to accompany the copy. This being tabloid fodder, *The Sun* would not be outdone. It responded by dredging up the transcript of a two-year-old phone conversation between Diana and her longtime friend, James Gilbey. Dubbed 'Squidgygate' by the red top paper that published it, the conversation actually read rather blandly. But with the eternal tabloid war suddenly heating up, a little detail like that was not going to keep the story out of print.

The year was shaping up to be a nightmare in terms of royal press, and not just because of the various marital disharmonies. There were not one but two significant breeches of Buckingham Palace's security. Just ten years after Michael Fagan had managed to get into Her Majesty's bedroom (while she was in it), another intruder success-fully made his way into the Palace gardens, while a short time later a second trespasser found his way through an open set of French doors and into the Palace itself.

While security breaches were a serious concern, it was still the human stories for which the public had an insatiable appetite. As the year drew to a close, it became increasingly obvious that the Waleses 11-year marriage was coming to an end.

I had always had my doubts that Prince Andrew's marriage was going to last, but the breakdown of the Waleses union saddened me. For all of the media's cynicism on the subject, I knew with certainty that at one point there had not only been a strong connection between the two, but genuine love and adoration.

Age difference aside, in the end I believe that Charles and Diana simply inhabited two different worlds.

CHAPTER 12

Trouble and Strife –
Annus Horribilis Part Two

November 1992

From the media's point of view, Charles and Diana's trip to South Korea in November of 1992 signalled the end of their marriage. I had travelled to Seoul ahead of the couple to carry out my usual pre-visit recce, and was on hand at the airport the day of their arrival. As the door to the aircraft opened I turned to the protection officer and said, 'we've lost this one.'

The Prince and the Princess were the epitome of Mr and Mrs Glum – her expression pinched and pale, his rigid and morose. Their body language was so hostile, it was as if they could have killed each other with a single glance, and the dark cloud hanging over them would remain throughout the tour.

Unless they were to her advantage, Diana had no interest in conducting joint tours anymore. She was much more concerned with undertaking solo visits, which were still few and far between. For the South Koreans, however, this was a valuable and significant visit. Regardless, the media's sole interest was of a more personal nature – how the royal couple was getting on…or, more to the point, *not* getting on. It was a tour in which the pictures alone told the story.

But one Household member's poor choice of words definitely didn't help matters.

'How are the Prince and Princess coping with all this?' asked *The Daily Mirror's* James Whitaker of the tour's private secretary. 'Is the marriage okay?'

'All marriages have their problems,' replied the private secretary, testily.

It was an attempt to deflect the question, but he pretty much gave credence to all the rumours that we had spent months trying to quash. If we hadn't lost the tour upon arrival, we had undoubtedly lost it now.

Indeed, less than a month after Their Royal Highnesses return to England, the then Prime Minister, John Major, announced to the House of Commons that the Prince and Princess of Wales had agreed to separate.

After years of speculation, the relief was palpable, but as one fire in the House of Windsor was extinguished, another, which would prove equally damaging, was about to ignite.

There has been a castle in Windsor for almost a thousand years. The longest occupied castle in Europe, it was built by William the Conqueror in the 11th century, following the Norman Conquest of 1066. Constructed as part of a defensive ring of motte and bailey castles around London (each a day's march from the other), it wasn't used as a royal residence until Henry I made it his home at the turn of the 12th century. Since then, it has been continuously occupied by royalty, sometimes as a main residence, such as when Queen Victoria lived there following the death of Prince Albert in 1861. At other times it served as a hunting lodge and party venue — as was the case with James I — or as a collection of grace-and-favour apartments for prominent widows and friends of the crown, as during the reign of George II.

Today, Windsor Castle is where the Queen spends the majority of her weekends throughout the year. Though she cherishes the peace and solitude of Balmoral, Windsor has always held fond family memories. The Queen and her sister, Princess Margaret, spent a large part of their childhood there during World War II. It had been suggested that the young princesses should be evacuated to Canada, but their mother refused, proclaiming, 'the children could not go without me, and I could not possibly leave the King…and the King will never leave.' For their safe keeping, the girls were sent to Windsor. There, they staged pantomimes at Christmas to raise money for The Queen's Wool Fund, which purchased yarn to knit military garments. Along with their nanny and governess, Elizabeth and Margaret sheltered in the castle dungeons during air raids. They also joined a local Girl Guide group, with whom they spent time alongside other evacuees.

Windsor continues to be a profoundly personal site for the Queen. Her parents are entombed in St George's Chapel, within the castle walls, along with the ashes of her sister Margaret.

Friday, 20th November, 1992 marked the Queen and Prince Philip's 45th wedding anniversary. There would be no celebrations, as the Prince was abroad on business. Instead the Queen would be heading to Windsor alone for the weekend.

I was in my office at Buckingham Palace when the phone rang. It was BBC Radio Berkshire.

'Can you confirm there's a fire at Windsor Castle?' asked the girl at the other end of the line.

This was news to me. Surely if it was true, someone would have phoned to inform the press office. I told her I couldn't confirm it, and that I would get back to her. I immediately called the Castle switchboard.

'Is there a fire there?'

'Erm, I can't tell you anything,' replied the operator.

'In that case, can you ask Major Eastwood to call me as soon as possible?' Major Jim Eastwood was the Superintendent of Windsor Castle at the time. If anyone was on the case, it would be he.

'I can't, I'm afraid. He's not here. He's a bit busy.'

Not surprising, given the news I'd just heard. I asked if she could get a message to him to call me, and then went to find Charles Anson.

I was standing in Anson's office and about to declare, 'There's a fire at Windsor Castle...' when the phone on his desk rattled to life with the news.

There was indeed a blaze raging through the Brunswick Tower, with 50-foot flames leaping into the sky. With the fire confirmed and a fervent media racing to the scene, Charles and I agreed that I should get to Windsor as quickly as possible. I sprinted out of the Palace and jumped into my car, switching on my hazard warning lights before tearing through the gates and making it to the Castle an impressive 28 minutes later.

Word of my imminent arrival had clearly preceded me, because when I swept in towards the advance gates I was ushered straight through. I followed the road up to the Quadrangle. The sight that greeted me was shocking. Flames ripped through the tower as police held back the swarms of correspondents.

My first task was to find a place where they would be able to report on the events as they unfolded without hampering the efforts of both the fire brigade and the military. After weighing the options, I relocated them to the Moat Path. It was an ideal location as it provided an unimpeded view of the fire and the accompanying activity in the Quadrangle, while also keeping them out of harm's way.

Fire engines descended in droves. Members of the armed forces had been drafted in from the two local barracks, Victoria and Cumbermere, to assist in moving to safety the many precious items from the Royal Collection.

In that respect, we had been very lucky. Longstanding work to replace the out-of-date wiring had been going on in that particular section of the Castle for some time. As a result, many of the treasures housed within its walls had already been cleared out. When the fire had finally been doused, we realised just how fortunate we had been. Only two major items in the Royal Collection were destroyed – an 18-foot Morel & Seddon sideboard, and a painting of George III by Sir William Beechey. Both works were of such vast dimensions that it was impossible to get them through the doorway.

The Queen arrived around 3pm. She was immediately met by Major Eastwood in the Quadrangle. He informed her that a halogen lamp had ignited a curtain in the Queen's Private Chapel at 11:33 that morning, and that the fire had proceeded to spread quickly to neighboring rooms. By 12:20pm, it had spread to St George's Hall, the largest of the State Apartments.

Prince Andrew, who'd been researching a project in the Castle's Royal Library, had immediately taken charge, assembling all able-bodied people to help evacuate works of art from the building. As Prince Charles rushed from Sandringham to aid in the rescue efforts, the Queen remained on site all day and into the evening. She would spend that night in her private apartment at the Castle, and return to assess the damage the following morning. In a largely unprecedented move, I had Andrew step before the cameras on two occasions to provide updates on the emergency personnel's progress. He was very good indeed.

The main fire continued to burn until 11 o'clock that night, and the secondary fires weren't completely extinguished until early Saturday morning.

The Windsor fire was the second conflagration in a royal residence in a short space of time. There had already been one at Hampton Court Palace in 1986, which had caused major damage to the King's Apartments, the restoration of which was only completed in 1990.

Being such a dramatic feature on the Windsor skyline, any destruction to the Castle would have had catastrophic implications. The fire was always going to be a major news story, and the scale of media interest was immense. What we couldn't have anticipated, however, was that an unguarded remark by a politician would lead to an even greater story.

The cost of the damage was estimated to be in the region of £40m. The following morning, as fire crews worked to dampen the remaining embers, the media posed a perfectly legitimate question: 'Who pays for the restoration'?

Secretary of State, Peter Brooke, an elected politician and member of the cabinet, went before the cameras, and in the heat of the moment announced, 'the government will pay.'

The outcry was vociferous and immediate, and the press enthusiastically fanned the flames of outrage and disgust.

I had been at the Castle managing the media throughout the crisis, as 225 firemen and emergency personnel struggled to contain the blaze, using over a million gallons of water from the River Thames. I had wrongly assumed that that would be my sole responsibility as press secretary, but a much more perilous job was to come. Within seconds, Peter Brooke, a government minister whose job it was to be absolutely non-committal, had handed the press a completely erroneous story on a platter.

Politicians are not very good at 'saying nothing'… unless it is they who are directly in the line of fire. With the statement now declared before a global audience, I was left to deal with a barrage of questions from what was becoming a very hostile press pack. The story gained momentum by the hour. It ran and ran. As head of the establishment, it was the Queen who was yet again left to carry the burden of responsibility. Nothing we said or did seemed to alter the public's perception or repair the damage. The media had struck at the weak underbelly of the Monarchy, and the press was going to run with it for as long as possible.

I have often wondered since what it must have felt like for the Queen at the time. A global royal news story with an ugly political twist must have been deeply traumatic for her. All that quite aside from the horror of watching her beloved home, which contained centuries of history, go up in smoke.

Four days later, on 24th November, Her Majesty gave a speech at the City of London's Guildhall. Already battling a heavy cold and laryngitis, she spoke sadly and eloquently of a year that she would, '...not look back on with undiluted pleasure. In the words of one of my more sympathetic correspondents,' she told the nation, 'it has turned out to be an *Annus Horribilis*.'

The question of who would pay for the Windsor Castle restoration wasn't just an opportunity to score party political points. It also highlighted just how much is misunderstood with regard to our Sovereign's wealth. Her Majesty's fortune has always been a matter of speculation. When *The Sunday Times* produced its first *Rich List* on 2nd April, 1989, it was clear that, as with most things royal-related, they were completely misguided. Predictably, they listed the Queen at number one. Why? They simply made an uninformed assumption.

What is now correctly understood is that Her Majesty does not have quite the property portfolio that the *Rich List* would have had us believe. She does not own all of the royal palaces and castles in the UK. In fact, she owns just two royal residences – the Sandringham Estate in Norfolk and Balmoral Castle in Scotland. The others are all owned by the State. When making the initial calculations, those charged with compiling the *Rich List* had thrown into the pot the Royal Navy's Royal Yacht *Britannia*, the RAF's Queen's Flight, the Royal Train, the Royal Collection (which the Queen merely holds in trust for her successors and the nation), and – erroneously – the Crown Jewels, which are also part of the Royal Collection. In short, her financial portfolio had been fabricated, and it took almost two years to convince *The Sunday Times* of the reality, which would prove to drop her down to a more realistic number 59 on the list.

By 2014 her place had fallen to 285, well behind Virgin Group founder, Sir Richard Branson (23), former Beatle Sir Paul McCartney (142), British composer and musical impresario Andrew Lloyd Webber (162) and *Harry Potter* creator JK Rowling (180).

Which begs the question: Why is the Queen dropping down the rankings year after year? The answer is actually very simple. Those above her are invariably involved in commercial, profit-making enterprises, with vast resources at their fingertips. Her Majesty solely has her investments. What these are, no one really knows, but they're certainly not as lucrative as some would have us think.

Meanwhile, I was about to see a big change in my own modest profit-making enterprise – my job. Unlikely as it may seem, the fire at Windsor Castle was about to play both a pivotal and ultimately positive role in my future.

CHAPTER 13

Receiving Visitors

August 1993

We hoped that the year following Her Majesty's *Annus Horribilis* would be significantly less dramatic. It proved to be a landmark year with a major and unexpected royal first.

While more than 50,000 people are invited to Buckingham Palace each year to attend state banquets, lunches, dinners, garden parties, investitures and receptions, the grounds had never been open to paying visitors. Aside from the necessary maintenance work that usually occurs during the summer months, there was no particular reason why it shouldn't have been opened to the public, especially given that the Queen and Prince Philip holiday at Balmoral in August and September each year.

Inspired by Her Majesty and endorsed by Prince Philip, the idea of a summer opening hoped to capitalize on those two available months in order to provide funding for the restoration of Windsor Castle.

The period following the Castle fire had been a

bruising one for the Royal Family, as indicated by the Queen's Christmas Day message that year, in which she stated: 'My heart goes out to those whose lives have been blighted by war, terrorism, famine, natural disaster or economic hardship. Like many other families, we have lived through some difficult days this year. The prayers, understanding and sympathy given to us by so many of you, in good times and bad, have lent us great support and encouragement. It has touched me deeply that much of this has come from those of you who have troubles of your own.'

Although some of the initial public fury died down in the wake of Her Majesty's speech, there were still public rumbles of dissatisfaction with a Monarchy continually perceived to be living the high life, while expecting taxpayers to fund the £40m restoration bill. A number of venomous letters detailing such frustrations made their way into print.

It would be an understatement to say that we in the press office felt aggrieved by what Peter Brooke had said on camera. Not only had he failed to consider the consequences of his actions, but he had also stood in defiance of his permanent secretary, Hayden Phillips, who had told Peter in no uncertain terms to withhold any information about how the rebuild was to be funded until details had been properly worked out.

With their backs against the wall, the Royals inevitably stuck to their guns and the public summer opening was put into place. The Palace called a media briefing on 29th April, 1993, at which it was announced that the State

Rooms would be opened to the public for a five-year experimental period. Entrance to the grounds of Windsor Castle – previously cost-free to visitors – would now be included as part of a new one-price ticket, replacing the previous ticket to tour the Castle itself. Minus startup costs, all revenues raised through admissions and souvenir sales would go directly into the restoration fund. The hope was that these measures would solicit 70 percent of the estimated £40m needed to repair the damaged areas of Windsor Castle.

The media was quick to praise the Monarch for such a revolutionary idea – a welcome turnaround from the previous weeks – but it wasn't long before praise turned to ridicule. Certain papers went on to lampoon the entire exercise, going so far as to make irreverent suggestions for the souvenirs that should be sold in the gift shops – *Kitsch at the Palace,* as one rag described it. Stuffed corgis, Prince Charles boxer shorts, royal loo roll covers and the like were loosely bandied about for consideration.

Frustrated at times by the response, though not at all surprised, we in the Household could do little but allow ourselves to be mildly amused by what we read. If anything, the ridicule only spurred us on to make the project work.

I had served five years as Press Secretary to the Prince and Princess of Wales, but their split inevitably necessitated an adjustment in my responsibilities. In February 1993, I accompanied Charles on a trip to Mexico. The previous November, just prior to the recce for that tour,

I'd received a call from Diana's private secretary, asking if I could accompany him on a recce to Paris, for the Princess's tour, scheduled for the same time as the Mexico trip. As I couldn't be in two places at once, a decision had to be made.

The circumstance would mark the end of my formal association with Diana, as I was left in charge of press management for the Prince alone.

Even before the issue with the tour schedules arose, I had discerned that some sort of change was imminent. It had been known for some time that the Prince wanted to break away from Buckingham Palace and create his own press office at St James's Palace, a move he planned to fund with revenues from the Duchy of Cornwall. His separation from the Princess presented him with the ideal opportunity to make the change sooner rather than later. The plan had actually been in the works just prior to the Windsor fire, and I knew that several members of staff would be involved in the reorganization. By the time they were redeployed, most had gone away satisfied with their new positions, or at the least, very grateful to still be in a job.

'His Royal Highness would like for you to continue working for him,' said the Prince's private secretary, Richard Aylard, when it came time for me to get the call.

There was just one snag. The move would mean my transferring from the Queen's Household, my current employer, to Charles's.

As soon as the offer came, I knew I didn't want to accept. Soon after beginning my career at the Palace, someone told me to 'never forget whose household you're in.' I had taken the advice to heart. I was a member of the Queen's Household, and felt tremendous loyalty to Her Majesty.

While I had nothing but respect for the heir to the throne, I declined his offer.

In theory, I was now out of a job. While the position hadn't been proposed as a 'go with the Prince or hop' offer, I had been left in the balance so to speak. A place needed to be found for me. That place would prove to be The Royal Collection.

As the department responsible for the care and maintenance of all the works of art under royal stewardship, as well as visitor management for Windsor Castle, it could not have been a more opportune time to join The Royal Collection. Following the fire, the department had suddenly found itself working in overdrive.

The summer opening of Buckingham Palace required an opening committee, which was duly assembled under the chairmanship of the Lord Chamberlain, Lord Airlie. Within that committee was the need for a new member of staff to oversee media relations, in short the committee's own dedicated press secretary. Enter yours truly.

In many ways it was a dream position. The Royal Collection had never had a designated press secretary, so I was able to create the role for myself with a blank canvas. As I saw it, there were three aspects to my new job. First, I would promote Royal Collection exhibitions in the Queen's Gallery at Buckingham Palace, as well as the exhibitions at Windsor Castle and the Palace of Holyrood House in Edinburgh.

Secondly, I would manage press interests in the Windsor Castle restoration. This entailed seeing to it that every element of rebuilding was recorded on film, both for archival purposes, and for the eventual production of a television documentary to be aired once the project was complete.

My final role would be to media-manage the Palace's summer opening. Following the emotional highs and lows of the past couple of years, not to mention the constant travelling, my new position was a welcome opportunity.

The first meeting of the summer opening committee took place in April. The Palace would open its doors to the public on 3rd August, immediately after the Queen's departure to Balmoral. There was much to be done within a short space of time.

Clearly, Buckingham Palace had not been designed to be a tourist attraction, so some strategic planning had to be implemented. It was decided that visitors would be permitted to see all of the State Rooms, which presented the logistical challenge of routing them in such a way as to avoid congestion and prevent them from having to retrace their steps. There was also the key business of making sure they were forced to exit by way of the yet-to-be-built gift shop. Then there were the peripheral matters: ticketing, public loos, souvenirs etc.

Naturally, security was also a major concern. At the outset, we knew we'd need a bag check and scanning equipment at the entrance. We would also need a marquee for the Ambassadors' Entrance on Buckingham Palace Road. Lastly, a small army of temporary wardens would need to be hired.

As a tour through the State Rooms presented an enormous amount of information for visitors to absorb, I suggested that we produce a half-hour video that would highlight the rooms' various features, and which could be purchased at the end of the tour.

Video production does not come cheap. I sought quotes from both British Ceremonial Arts (BCA) – the Palace's resident TV production company – as well as a number of out-of-house companies. The quotes ranged from £25,000 to £80,000.

'Ludicrous!' thundered one of the committee members who'd worked in television his entire life...only as an accountant rather than a producer. 'It's ridiculous to spend so much for something like this.'

He went on to suggest that I rent a hand-held video camera and film the various rooms myself.

'That's like asking an odd-job man to rebuild Windsor Castle!' I replied, offended by the suggestion. I emphatically declined.

The meeting room went silent. My gaze met that of the Lord Chamberlain, who was clearly stifling a smile.

I got my way.

The committee accepted BCA's quote of £25,000, and I duly produced the State Rooms documentary. I could only hope that my instinct would prove correct, and that sales would more than offset the cost.

Merchandising did not fall under my job detail, but the final selection of items to be sold in the gift shop would include bone china mugs and pill boxes, engraved glasses, coasters, commemorative plates and coins, Buckingham Palace-themed tea, biscuits and chocolate…and the inevitable guide book among other souvenirs.

By late spring, all that was left was to send out a press notice inviting reporters to a dedicated press day, which I felt would be the best way to reach out to the UK media as a whole. As a press office of one, it was a busy time for me.

I put together a comprehensive advisory that included all pertinent information about the project. It was sent to all of our contacts, as well as the Press Association – the UK's major news agency – under the assumption that through them it would also be picked up by the foreign news agencies.

We received more than 600 requests to attend. I personally answered each one with a hand written invitation. To my knowledge every one of them attended the press day, and experienced the inaugural tour of the magnificent State Rooms.

Joining some of the tours, I was stunned by the positive response from so many hardened, often cynical, journalists. Their approval became even more noticeable in the souvenir shop. Having laughed at our efforts earlier in the year, they proceeded to clear most of the shop's inventory. Panicked, we placed a much larger order of stock in preparation for opening to the general public. Our optimism was not displaced. The first year's summer opening was a phenomenal success, with over 400,000 visitors passing through the Palace gate. Our 'tacky' souvenirs sold like hotcakes, exceeding everyone's modest expectations.

In the years to come, our guidebook would go on to be printed in several languages. Even a simple Buckingham Palace carrier bag became a highly prized commodity. Personally, I was most thrilled to realise that we sold 15,000 copies of the documentary video at £10 per copy. It was £25,000 well spent.

With the first season of the Palace summer opening under my belt, there would soon be another royal residence preparing to admit visitors. In February 1994, my wife, daughter and I were offered the opportunity to move into a grace-and-favour apartment at Kensington Palace. Based in the Old Barracks, we were to live next door to the Queen's Private Secretary, Sir Robert Fellowes and his wife, Lady Jane – Diana's sister. Upstairs lived Brigadier Miles Hunt-Davis, Private Secretary to the Duke of Edinburgh, and his wife Gay, and Paul Burrell, Diana's infamous butler, shared the apartment opposite with his family. Ours was a cosy two-bedroom flat with ample space for the three of us. At first it was strange to live so close to where I worked, but it was also incredibly convenient. My previous 45-minute slog through heavy traffic had become a ten-minute drive or a half-hour leisurely stroll on foot to Buckingham Palace.

Diana may not have been my boss any longer, but living just down the road from her gave me the opportunity to continue to see her on a regular basis.

CHAPTER 14

Smiling for the Cameras

June 1994

By the end of 1992, the public's perception of Prince Charles could not have been worse. He was increasingly portrayed as the villain, while Diana – thanks largely to the Andrew Morton memoir (which she continued to deny having had anything to do with) – was generally viewed as the victim. Charles could do nothing but keep his head down and continue with his responsibilities as heir to the throne.

In 1993, he agreed to do a televised interview for an ITV documentary detailing the various achievements of his exceedingly successful charity, The Prince's Trust. I thought the program would serve as an ideal vehicle in which to shift focus away from his personal life and back to more worthy matters.

As so often happens with best-laid schemes, things quickly went awry. What was supposed to be a straightforward, strictly work-related interview turned into something much more personal, as Charles was coaxed into baring his soul on the issue of his failed marriage to Diana.

Filmed in part in the choir stalls of St George's Chapel, Windsor, the interview proved excruciating at times, as the Prince openly confessed to his extramarital affair with Camilla Parker Bowles. Perhaps equally damaging was the Prince's contention that, while he was not considering divorce at the time, he did not believe that it would present a barrier to his becoming King. Once he ascended the throne, Charles would serve as Supreme Governor of the Church of England and Defender of the Faith, and this was at a time when divorce was still a highly contentious issue in many religious quarters.

I have no doubt that Richard Aylard, the Prince's Private Secretary, had persuaded Charles to answer the questions. Interviewer Jonathan Dimbleby would have certainly provided additional influence. Whatever the case, the piece aired in June 1994, just shy of the 25th anniversary of his investiture as Prince of Wales. Charles was met with a firestorm of commentary from armchair pundits and faced criticism across the board. Regrettably, nearly all mention of The Prince's Trust – a fine institution, and the overriding subject of the documentary as it was originally proposed – was lost in the scandal.

Combustible as the Morton book and Dimbleby interview had been, down in the press office, we couldn't help but believe that all of Charles and Diana's 'dirty laundry' had finally been aired, and that some sense of normality could one again be established within the Royal Household. We could not have been more wrong.

On 20th November, 1995 (the Queen and Prince Philip's 48th wedding anniversary), Diana – ever eager to have the last word – fired a final shot, appearing in a televised tell-all interview with Martin Bashir for the BBC's news magazine programme *Panorama*.

As was the Princess's intention, neither the Press Office nor the Royal Household at large knew anything about the interview prior to its airing. Only Patrick Jephson, the Princess's private secretary, had received any hint. Diana had indicated to him that she had done the interview, but revealed nothing about its contents, telling him only, 'Don't worry, everything will be all right.'

The BBC was positively covert in keeping the programme under wraps, which only served to ensure a vast viewing audience. Not even Lord Hussey, chairman of the BBC Governors, knew anything about the interview beforehand. Perhaps producers had kept him in the dark because his wife, Lady Susan, served as a Lady-in-Waiting to the Queen.

Bracing for the worst, we in the press office crowded around the television in Charles Anson's office to watch the broadcast. Most of the press and private secretaries were there, around six of us in total. With the exception of the occasional sharp intake of breath, we watched the interview unfold with silent, rapt attention.

Diana withheld nothing.

'There were three of us in this marriage,' she told Bashir, 'so it was a bit crowded.' She went on to admit that she'd been in love with James Hewitt, and confirmed that she had been unfaithful to the Prince.

Diana would later confide to friends that she regretted doing the interview. The consequences were entirely as I had expected. The media simply couldn't get enough of it, splashing her face on magazine covers around the world and filling airwaves with provocative sound bites. Through it all, Diana somehow managed to conduct business as usual. Three days after the *Panorama* interview aired, she left without a backward glance for an official visit to Argentina with her private secretary. The inevitable fallout was left for those back home to deal with...although not all of them did.

Geoff Crawford, Diana's press secretary, resigned immediately. Her Private Secretary, Patrick Jephson, followed soon after, handing in his notice upon their return from South America. Both men cited a lack of trust as the basis for their resignation, claiming that if she couldn't take them into her confidence, then there was no point in continuing a working relationship that necessitated a close, personal level of communication.

Admittedly, I too was displeased by Diana's actions, believing that in many respects it reflected a monumental lack of judgment. I was also dismayed that people who perhaps didn't have her best interests at heart had managed to talk her into doing something so damning.

And it wasn't just she who had been affected. The institution of the Monarchy, her extended family and, most importantly, her children, were also made to answer for the Princess's transgressions. Indeed, as one reporter put it, her interview had, 'plunged the Monarchy into the greatest crisis since the Abdication.'

It must be said that I was also deeply saddened by what I saw and heard in the *Panorama* piece. I knew from experience how difficult a crumbling marriage could be. It is something I can't imagine having to endure under a global spotlight. Granted, Diana delivered a masterful performance, but I also couldn't help but be moved by the authentic vulnerability and pain exhibited throughout the interview. At the end of the day, the woman who had sat down with Martin Bashir was a devoted young mother who had suffered the prolonged and heartbreaking disintegration of her marriage, and who now seemed to be, above all, lonely.

Meanwhile, much of my own attention was turned to the issues of the Palace's non-human assets, which certainly made for a more harmonious workday. My main concern at the time was overseeing the filming of the on-going restoration at Windsor Castle, with the in-house television crew gathering footage several times a week to document the progress.

I also kept a close eye on the restoration itself, conferring with the specialists involved to ensure that the project continued to run smoothly. As chairman of the restoration committee, the Duke of Edinburgh was a regular visitor to the work site, and we spoke frequently. Very much hands-on, Prince Philip was chiefly responsible for the design of the new stained glass window that was to be installed in the chapel.

I enjoyed being so involved in the Windsor restoration project, but other royal assets also commanded my attention. One such asset was the Royal Collection of fine art. Spread throughout the various palaces, and having been amassed over centuries from artists spanning the globe, it is the largest and most famous private collection of artworks in the world.

There is estimated to be over a million separate items in the Royal Collection, and the Queen takes her role as its custodian very seriously. She has lived with it for 88 years, and as a result has a deep respect for every piece. While she is not an art historian, she is extremely well educated about a significant number of the items. In terms of inventory, she knows that there are 3,000 objects on permanent loan to museums and galleries in the UK; she knows where the majority of the paintings within the collection are on display, and if a particular painting is missing from its usual spot, she will notice immediately. She has a very good sense of what is included in the Royal Archives and the Royal Library at Windsor, and she could tell you all about the object that decorate the State Banquet table.

In terms of artistic theory and appreciation, Her Majesty can hold her own with anyone, possessing an almost encyclopedic knowledge about a number of different art forms and techniques.

Contrary to popular belief, the Queen does not own the Collection; she holds it in trust for her successors and the nation, which is why so much of it is on public display in all of the royal palaces, as well as in museums and galleries. Because she doesn't own any of the pieces, she can't sell any of them.

Towards the end of 1995, it was decided that a number

of paintings from the collection would be sent on an overseas tour to New Zealand, Australia and Canada the following January. Some 30 paintings were chosen, all of them priceless, by such notable artists as Van Dyck, Rembrandt, Stubbs, Winterhalters and Agasse.

The National Gallery of Australia suggested that a knowledgeable representative accompany the paintings in order to speak about them while they were on display. It was agreed, as I had broadcast experience, and might therefore have the necessary tools to avoid boring the pants off of viewers with a slew of curatorial jargon, that I was the obvious choice to send.

The only problem was that I knew bugger all about art.

I fear that this was a rather transparent detail, as one day while walking down Palace Avenue, Diana hooted and pulled her car alongside me to ask how I was enjoying my new position at The Royal Collection. She followed up by asking with a grin, 'what the fuck to you know about art?'

While I can be a master bluffer at times, it was clear that I had some boning up to do.

Prior to the trip, I familiarized myself with the backgrounds and styles of the paintings I would be exhibiting. *The Young Card Players,* a 17th century French work by one of the Le Nain brothers (no one can confirm which), depicted a group of boys clustered around a table playing *primero,* an early form of poker. Now this was something I could talk about...at least with more authority than lilies or fig leaves.

The work would become my principal subject. I read as much as I could about it and its creator(s). I noted that the painting was generally described as being 'Caravaggesque,' which I found to be a good word – the sort of word that a press secretary-cum-art expert could bandy about with admirable dominion – so I filed it away to wheel out when necessary.

As I continued to put myself through Art School 101, the paintings were sent away for cleaning in preparation for display. Shortly after their return, Christopher Lloyd, Surveyor of the Queen's Pictures, approached me in the press office.

'You'll never guess what!'

'What?' I asked, somewhat concerned. I had already been scheduled to promote the exhibition on various Australian television programs, and Christopher knew about my fear of being caught out as an unknowledgeable imposter. Had they decided to send him instead?

That wasn't the case.

'You know *The Young Card Players?*' he said. 'Turns out there's a woman in it too!'

Indeed the card-playing boys had miraculously swelled their ranks. The cleaning process, an art form in itself, had led to the discovery of another character in the painting – a woman, standing in the background looking on. More interestingly, it was determined that the female figure had been painted over sometime in the 18th century. But there was more. The bandage on one of the boy's heads had disappeared. So, too, had the artist's signature.

It was ultimately determined that the painting was a fake – a successful attempt to pass off the work as a Caravaggio...so successful, in fact, that when it was purchased by George IV, then the Prince of Wales, he thought that he was buying a canvas painted by the famed legendary Baroque artist.

For a Surveyor of the Queen's Pictures, I could well understand how this could be a source of great excitement. As an art imbecile, soon expected to wax lyrical on the subject with estimable profundity, I was over the moon. I now had a story – something concrete to talk about, which would hopefully interest viewers even more than discussions of brush strokes and tonal values.

The tour also allowed for a fortunate personal coincidence. My daughter, Victoria, had recently played Snow White in a theatrical production in Newcastle, and had gone on to tour with Disney in Paris, Dubai and Kuwait. Now, she was making an even bigger leap.

'I've applied to drama school,' she told me, just a couple of weeks before my trip.

'Where?'

'New York!' she exclaimed. 'You can take me to my audition on your way to Australia.'

I had naturally assumed that she would apply to a school in London, but she had clearly inherited her father's wanderlust. Would she ever come home to the UK again? Instinct told me that she might not.

Still, I greeted this news with tremendous joy. I did indeed accompany her to the audition before flying on to Sydney. Victoria went on to ace her audition, and accepted a coveted scholarship at the American Academy of Dramatic Arts in New York. I could not have been more proud.

That's not to say that it was an easy adjustment for me. I had relinquished the parental reins a couple of years earlier, but there would be a world of difference in having my little girl an ocean away, as opposed to a couple of tube stops.

Victoria had been just three-and-a-half when my first marriage ended. Aside from the help of a string of au pairs, I raised her as a full-time single dad.

Emotionally, I was not able to accompany her on her permanent move to New York. I was thrilled that she was moving to a good place, and that she was so keen to get there. But with her departure stirring up so many of my own unhappy memories – of being dropped off, motherless and terrified, at boarding school – I simply did not trust myself to go with her on that second trip. Victoria and I said our farewells at Heathrow, and my wife went to New York with her instead. I would have only cried throughout the entire journey.

Not for nothing is such a moment called a watershed.

CHAPTER 15

Death of a Princess: Diana –
The Longest Week

August 31ˢᵗ 1997

I t is an inescapable fact that sometimes people die young. It doesn't matter who you are, where you live, your race, nationality or creed, the spectre of untimely death is simply a tragic fact of life, and when such a tragedy occurs, we are never less than shocked to the core.

Just as everyone remembers where they were when President Kennedy was assassinated, or when the planes flew into the twin towers of the World Trade Center in New York, so too can almost everyone recall where they were when the news broke, at 12:30am French time on August 31ˢᵗ, 1997, that Diana, Princess of Wales, and her friend, Dodi Fayed, had been involved in a serious car accident in Paris.

I was in my apartment at Kensington Palace. Like most people at that hour, I was in bed. I had only just turned out the light and was dropping off to sleep when the high-pitched beep of my radio pager jolted me awake.

I was used to my beeper going off at all times of the day

and night; it came with the territory. With a responsibility to media organisations around the world, many of which were located in different time zones, there were often calls during anti-social hours, but I knew that the first editions of the Sunday papers had already dropped, so I was baffled as to whom could be paging me at such a late hour.

I fumbled around the bedside table for my pager and read the display telling me to call CNN in Atlanta. Given the time difference, US networks often called late, but August is generally a quiet month due to the Royal Family being on holiday. We considered it 'silly season' for any stories relating to the Monarchy, so a call at such a late hour this time of year was unusual. I grabbed my mobile and made the call.

'Can you tell me about the crash in Paris?' an American voice asked.

'Crash?' I asked. 'What crash?

I tried to gather my thoughts. *What on earth were they on about? Paris? What kind of crash?*

'The one involving Princess Diana,' he clarified.

The words hit their mark. Bang. I was suddenly wide-awake and heading for the living room to turn on the television. *What could have possibly happened?*

'I think you had better phone the duty press secretary at Buckingham Palace,' I told the reporter.

I knew that if anything untoward had happened involving a member of the Royal Family, the duty press secretary would have been informed.

I turned on the television and switched immediately to CNN to find out for myself. Diana had been involved in a major high-speed car crash in the Pont de l'Alma tunnel in the centre of Paris. French police had confirmed that her friend, Dodi Fayed, and the car's driver, Henri Paul, had been pronounced dead at the scene. Diana and her bodyguard, Trevor Rees-Jones, had been taken to hospital with serious injuries, and the members of the paparazzi who had been pursuing the car had been arrested.

It was too surreal to take in.

Diana arrived at Pitié-Salpêtrière Hospital at 2:06am. Despite lengthy resuscitation attempts, her internal injuries were simply too severe, and she was pronounced dead at 4:00am, French time — three-and-a-half-hours after I received the initial call from CNN. She was 36.

I was horrified, and gripped by an overwhelming sense of loss.

How could she be dead?

Could it be possible that I would no longer see her speed up the private road to Kensington Palace? No longer get a hello and a friendly wave if I happened to bump into her? It was deeply upsetting. While I knew I had to keep abreast of what was happening, I could hardly bear to watch. I also knew that I had to push my emotions to one side. I had a job to do. Within half an hour of receiving confirmation of the Princess's death, I was at my desk in the Buckingham Palace press office.

I arrived just before 4am BST, closely followed by deputy press secretary to the Queen, Penny Russell-Smith. As Penny went to find the duty private secretary, I got on the phone to the Keeper of the Privy Purse and the

Managing Director of Royal Collection Enterprises. It was the height of the tourist season, meaning Buckingham Palace, Windsor Castle and Holyrood House would all be open to the public, and I needed to let them know what had happened in case they wanted to remain closed for the day.

The press office phones were ringing off the hook, and it wasn't long before the switchboard was jammed with incoming calls. We did the best we could, agreeing to a holding line that, 'arrangements were still under discussion and that we would have more information later that morning.' For expediency we told them that any updates would be passed along to the Press Association, whom we would inform with updates as they became available. For once, journalists and broadcasters accepted the situation. They backed off and waited along with the rest of the world.

The next task was to deal with the flagpoles atop all of the royal buildings. I phoned the superintendents at Windsor Castle and Edinburgh's Holyrood House, as well as the factor at the Queen's private home, Sandringham House, in Norfolk, and asked them to lower their flags to half-mast. There was no need to do the same with the government buildings, as they already had a system in place. Upon the death of any member of the Royal Family, they automatically lower the Union Flag to half-mast.

The question of what to do at Buckingham Palace was another matter. With Her Majesty in residence at Balmoral, there was no flag currently flying over the Palace. As tradition dictates, the Royal Standard only flies there when the sovereign is in residence. It has been the case since 1837, when Queen Victoria acceded and took up residence.

Here was the conundrum; the Royal Standard is never flown at half-mast, even when the sovereign passes away. Many will be familiar with the term, 'The King is Dead, Long Live the Queen!' The tradition of the flag is that sentiment encapsulated.

The same rule does not apply to other royal homes. When the Queen is not in residence at Windsor Castle or Holyrood House in Edinburgh, a flag is still flown – the Union Flag and Scottish Saltire respectively.

But Buckingham Palace was a problem. Do we fly a flag at half-mast when traditionally no flag should be flown at all? Fly a Union Flag when tradition dictates the Royal Standard? Or just leave the pole glaringly bare? These were questions which, in the dawn hours of 31st August, 1997 no-one seemed capable of answering.

Household from the Lord Chamberlain's Office began to arrive around 6am. They were charged with organizing ceremonial occasions and funerals, and would ultimately be responsible for drawing up the guest list for Diana's funeral, as well as sending out all the invitations.

Funerals for members of the Royal Family are almost always planned well in advance. With full cooperation and input from the principal concerned, decisions are made ahead of time regarding the type of arrangements they would like. This was the case for virtually every member of the Royal Family, but it seemed no-one had actually taken the time to discuss plans with Diana. While married to

Prince Charles, she was still so young that perhaps it didn't seem like a priority, but now there was the additional issue that, as she had lost her royal title due to her divorce, she was, in theory, no longer considered a member of the Royal Family.

With no plans in place, nor a model to follow, we were left answering questions on the fly. The number one priority was deciding exactly what type of funeral Diana should have. Everything rested on the final decision. Diana, Princess of Wales, as she was now officially known, was, in effect, a private citizen. As such, she was entitled to a private citizen's funeral – i.e. one without any input from the Royal Household. It was a judgment that ultimately lay with Earl Spencer, Diana's brother and head of the Spencer Family, who was based in Cape Town, South Africa.

By 10am we had a verdict from the Earl. Though technically not a royal matter, he had decided that as the mother of a future king, and a globally popular public figure, his sister should have a royal funeral.

Leaving his devastated sons with their grandparents at Balmoral, Prince Charles had flown from Aberdeen to RAF Brize Norton in Oxfordshire to meet Diana's sisters, Lady Jane Fellowes and Lady Sarah McCorquodale. They would fly to Paris aboard a BAe 146 from No. 32 The Royal Squadron, to bring the Princess home.

From five o'clock that morning, members of the public had begun to lay flowers at the Palace gates. They came in their droves to share their grief and pay their respects, but as the number of bouquets escalated, so too did the concerns of those responsible for the changing of the guard.

The guard commander dispatched a policeman to let us know that the proliferation of flowers outside the centre gates was a problem. Traditionally used by the outgoing guard, the gates would need to be kept unobstructed later that morning.

On a normal day that would be reasonable, but this was not a normal day.

'I'm sorry but that's not going to be an option,' I told the policeman.

Within minutes, the guard commander came to see me himself. Either he was unaware of the enormity of what had happened in Paris in the early hours of that morning, or he was not quite conversant with what seemed to be unquestionably the right thing to do. It would look appalling if we were seen to be clearing the flowers out of the way. I was surprised he couldn't see that for himself.

I told him in no uncertain terms that he would have to find a way to work around the situation. The flowers were staying.

'That's going to be complicated,' he argued, before explaining just how difficult it would be to arrange. I got angry. It seemed like such an inappropriate line to take. I told him there were three other gates that could be used, and that the flowers would not be moved.

It was 10:30am. With the matter resolved, I set off for RAF Northolt to begin the process of coordinating the media for Diana's return journey home.

The RAF had an operational plan in place for transporting a royal casket, but it was a plan that had never been rehearsed, let alone put into practice. As I drove the 15 miles from central London to the air base, I could only trust in the professionalism of the armed forces to see to it that everything progressed without a hitch.

Arriving just after 11am, I went straight into an operational meeting led by the station commander. There, I was reassured that the same protocols as written down on paper were being exercised. The time at which the Princess's body would be released from the hospital to her family members had been sent through from Paris, and everything appeared to be in order.

One aspect the commander hadn't planned on, and which I was all too aware of – as I was about to get in touch with the Press Association and all the networks to inform them of the schedule – was the sheer number of journalists that would be present to cover the arrival of BAe 146 and its precious cargo.

It was just as well that the RAF was on the case so quickly and efficiently, attending to every crucial detail such as where the aircraft should stop, how much space it would need to turn around and, as a consequence, where the media pen should to be situated. As dozens of people, vehicles, and equipment would be descending upon the base on what would otherwise have been a quiet Sunday, a number of accommodations had to be rushed into place. Refreshments had to be brought in and rigorous security measures had to be taken – both difficult feats given the lack of advanced notice. Finally, clearing the terminal and apron required shifting various sets of loading steps and a couple of generators.

All the while, I stood in preparation for what would be the most important press briefing of my career.

The sadness in the still summer air that Sunday was palpable. A convoy of vehicles carrying military, security and broadcasting personnel began arriving at the allotted hour. For a time, all transports would be held in a secure area before being permitted on to the airfield proper.

The RAF had made a hangar available for my briefing to the media. As reporters and photographers arrived, there was none of the usual lighthearted banter. No shouting, no laughter and no noisy clatter of equipment.

Among the some 300 members of the press in attendance, I saw a sea of familiar faces: James Whitaker and Kent Gavin of *The Mirror*, Arthur Edwards from *The Sun*, Ian Jones from *The Telegraph* and John Stillwell from the Press Association. Also present were freelance photographers Tim Graham, Jane Fincher, Anwar Hussein and Robin Nunn, as well as Brian Hanrahan and Nicholas Witchell from the BBC, to name but a few. I had known them all for many years. Their faces all bore the same stunned and sad expression.

They all knew each other, too. It's not called a press 'pack' for nothing. Although they quietly conversed, everyone seemed diligently focused on getting through the next few hours as professionally – and reverently – as possible.

The relationship between a royal correspondent and a member of the Royal Family is a personal one. Here was a crowd which had covered every intimate aspect of Diana's adult life. From her marriage and the birth of her two sons, to countless royal tours and her ultimate divorce and its aftermath, they had witnessed the Princess's every high and low. Breaking news on this type of scale is the 'Holy Grail' to reporters, but none of them ever imagined that they would be covering her death.

I borrowed a photographer's ladder and climbed to the top step.

'We know why we're here, don't we?' I began.

The press briefing went without incident. Professionalism was the order of the day and the questions that would normally have been fired from all angles were conspicuously absent. It was clear that no-one had yet come to terms with the events of the day. All seemed quite clear about the ground rules for the homecoming. There was to be no littering of film boxes, no noise, no shouting or jockeying for position, and a blanket ban on motorized cameras.

An even greater silence fell at 6:30pm, when the assembled media were escorted out to the press pen. All gazes moved expectantly towards the sky, awaiting the first glimpse of the tell-tale aircraft lights. It didn't matter where anyone stood, as they would all have an unimpeded view. Silence reigned across the entire base. Even the arrival of Prime Minister Tony Blair caused little stir.

The plane came into view just before seven. The only movement was that of camera lenses pointing skyward as the wing lights grew brighter with the aircraft's gradual approach to landing.

Upon landing, the plane taxied away from view, and it was some time before it appeared again, as, prior to its return, the casket had to be turned around inside the hold in order to be carried out by the pallbearers. The aircraft eventually came to a stop outside the terminal building, and the high-pitched whine of the engines gave way to silence.

The media's presence was hardly felt. There was none of the usual machine gun-like rattle of motor-drives as the Lord Chamberlain, head of the Queen's household, walked to the foot of the steps to greet the Prince of Wales and Diana's sisters, who took their places alongside the other dignitaries gathered in front of the plane.

The bearer party from the Queen's Colour Squadron, RAF Regiment, formed up at the starboard rear cargo door. Draped with the Royal Standard, the casket emerged to an eerie calm. None of us could quite accept what we were seeing as the pallbearers gathered the casket onto their shoulders and moved at a slow march to the awaiting hearse. As my eyes began to water, the true gravity of what I was witnessing fully began to set in.

With the exception of the bowed heads and salutes, there was little ceremony. Within minutes, the assembled party had dispersed and gone their separate ways. Prince Charles immediately flew back to his sons in Scotland. The hearse, followed by a suite car carrying the Princess's sisters and Lt. Col. Anthony Mather, began its slow journey to London. The Princess was to be taken to a mortuary in Fulham, before making her next journey to the Chapel Royal at St James's Palace, where she would lie until the time came to lay her to rest.

After staying on to answer the remaining press queries, I left the base about 30 minutes behind the hearse, to make my own journey back to London. The airport perimeter was still thronged by the crowd which had gathered to witness the plane's arrival. As I drove up the M40, the westbound carriageway was still at a standstill as passengers had disgorged from their cars to stand and watch the cortege pass by. That they were still there, a half hour later, reflected a hint of the outpouring of public grief that was to come.

Back in central London, things were moving at a much quicker pace. From my car window I saw that the banks of flowers and mementoes were continuing to build up outside Buckingham Palace, as were the queues to sign the books of condolence we'd quickly arranged to be placed in St James's Palace.

Upon returning to my desk at the press office, I began to sense the scope of what duties lay ahead in the coming days. I was informed that there would be a planning meeting at 10am the following morning, and turned my attention to the necessary media-related preparations. Questions regarding the impending funeral were flooding in from all fronts. I answered them as best I could with whatever knowledge I was able to offer at the time.

It was almost midnight before I returned home to Kensington Palace – a routine that would continue until the day of the funeral. While I'd been profoundly moved by the sight of the Princess's casket emerging from the aircraft, I was still so immersed in the tasks at hand, that I'd allowed myself no time to properly grieve the loss that

I felt. In short, I'd consciously flipped the switch in my brain that would keep me in work mode, and resolutely forced myself to stay in that state for the remainder of the day.

It had been 22 hours since I'd left Kensington Palace, and it was only upon seeing the sight that greeted me when I arrived back at home that the enormity of Diana's loss to the world became readily apparent.

The flowers in particular were a sight to behold – a steadily growing carpet of color completely obscuring the vast stretch of grass that extended from the Kensington Palace railings. Their scent was overwhelming. Heightening the effect was the low buzz from the assembled crowd, which had remained to keep vigil in spite of the late hour. Their unashamed weeping could be heard in every direction, each of them united in their collective shock and grief. Every walk of life was represented – young couples, mothers with little ones, men in smart suits with briefcases, elderly gents and teenagers. Most had probably never even seen Diana in the flesh, and yet their empathy was intense.

Diana had always said that she wanted to be a princess of people's hearts…and in death, it was clear that she was.

CHAPTER 16

The Biggest Global Media
Event Ever

Monday, 1ˢᵗ September, 1997

Monday dawned all too quickly, and preparations for the Princess's funeral began in earnest.

Before returning to my apartment at Kensington Palace the previous night, I had been to Canada Gate to check on the arrangements for the media. I found that my worst fears had been realised. Though the Royal Family was not in residence, the press was obviously anticipating its imminent return to London.

In response to the continuing pilgrimage to Kensington Palace by members of the public, and in expectation of the Queen's much-speculated upon arrival at Buckingham Palace, a sprawling, disorganized media camp had begun to take shape in Green Park. I knew it would need to be contained and overseen, and I was greatly relieved when the Royal Parks department said that it would handle the arrangements. Clearly we were still only just beginning to grasp the full scale of the event.

Overnight the Lord Chamberlain, Lord Airlie, and his team had made many of the big decisions, and now it was a case of rolling out the plans and putting them into action. Time was of the essence.

The first of what would prove to be a daily meeting leading up to the funeral itself was held in the Chinese Dining Room in Buckingham Palace, and was led by the Lord Chamberlain. Some two-dozen key personnel were present, including the relevant private and press secretaries and government officials from the prime minister's office. Among them were John Holmes, Angie Hunter and Alastair Campbell. Also in attendance were the Metropolitan Police Commissioner, Paul Condon, Assistant Commissioner, Anthony Speed, the permanent secretary to the Department for Culture, Media and Sport (DCMS), Hayden Phillips, and, on conference call from several hundred miles away at Balmoral, the Queen's deputy private secretary, Robin Janvrin.

While there was no funeral plan approved by the Princess, there *was* a format for royal funerals in London, and a defined ceremonial route from the Chapel Royal in St James's Palace to Westminster Abbey. This was duly discussed and agreed upon, contrary to the media-driven spin that gave the impression that the government had masterminded the plans. The only contribution the government made to the proceedings was a blank cheque covering the costs.

The date was also set. The funeral would take place on Saturday, 6th September, which gave us less than five days to put everything into place. We were told that it would take the form of a 'non-ceremonial royal funeral', which left almost everyone around the table none the wiser.

Once explained, it turned out to be very simple. A service would be held in Westminster Abbey, and the route would follow the same path set for 'Tay Bridge.'

The word 'Tay' in this particular instance refers to the Queen Mother. The context of the word 'bridge' is rather lovely. Each individual royal funeral plan has the suffix 'bridge' attached to it. It is used to denote the deceased's final journey – bridging the gap between life on earth and the hereafter.

It was decided that Diana's procession would follow the same path as the funeral planned for the Queen Mother. It would leave the Chapel Royal, travel down The Mall, up Horse Guards Approach Road, across Horse Guards Parade Ground, though the arch of HQ London District, Horse Guards building, and turn right into Whitehall, before processing on to the Abbey. The interment would then take place in the Spencer Family vault at Great Brington, near to the family home at Althorp House.

In essence, the term 'non-ceremonial' meant that there would be less pomp and pageantry than there would have been had the Princess still been married to Prince Charles – no marching military, no bands and no street liners, which collectively was at least one less element to worry about. There would, however, be a gun carriage from the King's Troop Royal Horse Artillery to bear the coffin, accompanied by a bearer party from the Welsh Guards.

The final item on the agenda that morning was the

matter of the guest list for the service, but as it was to be collated by the Princess's office, the meeting was able to adjourn and we were all able to crack on with our various responsibilities. The burden of time weighed heavily on all our shoulders. We had less than five days to organise what would be the biggest royal event since the Princess's wedding 16 years earlier – something that took at least twice as many months to plan.

Behind Canada Gate, workers toiled rapidly to construct the commentary boxes – similar to those built for the start of the summer openings four years earlier – to house the broadcasters. My part in the proceedings was now clear. I was to manage the press for what was proving to be the biggest international media event in royal history. While Penny was tasked with updating the newly-launched royal website, detailing the arrangements for the funeral, I got in touch with the DCMS, which was coordinating the press positions along the planned route and at Church House, which would also be providing facilities for a full media briefing three days hence.

In the short term, I needed to convene a meeting with the various networks – BBC Television and Radio, ITN, Sky and IRN – so that I could explain the proposed route, along with details and timings.

The irony of what we were doing was not lost on any member of the team. Only ten days previously, we had walked the exact same route, discussed the exact same plans and agreed upon the exact same terms for the Queen Mother's funeral. We never imagined we would be doing it so soon after, for another royal entirely, one for whom we never could have predicted such a tragedy.

Still, for want of a blessing, it was helpful to have everything so fresh in our minds. It was also reassuring that, true to their word, the Royal Parks department seemed to be managing the media encampment that was growing in Green Park by the hour.

So far so good. But perhaps there was something we *could* have predicted – that something had to give.

It was all going too easily.

Tuesday, 2ⁿᵈ September, 1997

Tuesday's morning meeting was once again held in the Chinese Dining Room, and as was the case the previous day, it began with many questions. It was becoming apparent that there were a couple of elephants in the room that needed addressing as a matter of priority, namely: Why hadn't the Queen returned to speak to her people, and why was there no flag flying at half-mast over Buckingham Palace?

The nation was still in a state of shock about the Princess's death. The evidence was all around us in the escalating mountains of flowers, candles and cuddly toys, the sheer numbers of people streaming into the capital to pay their respects, and the headlines that were beginning to appear on television and in the papers declaring that the people wanted their Monarch back, and they wanted it to happen now.

We, of course, knew the facts. The Queen and her

family were dealing with the tragedy in their own private way. Her Majesty's primary concern was protecting Princes William and Harry from the glare of the media spotlight, and from the unprecedented number of grieving masses flooding into London – all sights for which the boys would have to brace themselves when the time came to return home. Amidst the outpouring of public sorrow over the woman the Prime Minister had dubbed the 'People's Princess', it was easy to forget that there were two bereaved children involved...but not by Her Majesty. She was determined to stay with her grandsons for as long as she possibly could.

It was becoming rapidly apparent that the media were not happy with the Queen's notable absence. Hard on the heels of the negative press surrounding the Waleses divorce, the decision was seen as inappropriate in some quarters. *'SPEAK TO US, MA'AM,'* thundered one paper. *'YOUR PEOPLE ARE SUFFERING,'* wailed another. *'SHOW US YOU CARE,'* demanded a third. Such headlines only served to whip up yet more negative public opinion, underlining the media-led common belief that our Royal Family was getting it wrong, and was distinctly out of touch.

It needed addressing, but once the conference link to Balmoral was established, the comments from the deputy private secretary were not positive. The Queen still had no immediate plans to travel to London, and her secretary was apparently also struggling with the requests to fly a Union Flag at half-mast over Buckingham Palace, and whether to have all the male members of the Royal Family walk behind the gun carriage. It has long been tradition for royal males with a military connection to walk behind the gun carriage at a royal funeral, but I think everyone was in agreement that the two young Princes, aged only 12 and 15, should be excused. To have to endure walking through the streets of London, lined with wailing masses, following their mother's funeral procession, must have felt nigh on impossible to them.

But it was Prince Philip who made a deal with his grandsons saying, 'If I walk will you both walk?' They agreed. I don't doubt that as the years have passed, they feel profoundly grateful to have found the strength to do so.

In terms of other walkers, it was my colleague, Penny Russell-Smith, who came up with the inspired suggestion that, as there wouldn't be the usual royal ceremonial components, it might be appropriate to invite representatives from some of the Princess's many charities to walk behind the gun carriage as part of the funeral procession.

The idea was adopted immediately, as was my own suggestion of finding a way to include the tens of thousands of people who would be flocking to the capital, but who, due to sheer numbers, would be unlikely to see the procession themselves. I proposed deploying loudspeakers along the route, so that people could hear the funeral service, and to erect a giant screen in Hyde Park so that other spectators could watch the event as it unfolded.

The police were so enthused by this idea that they suggested we go one step further and put up a screen in Regent's Park as well. I disagreed.

'I don't think people will go there,' I argued. 'Almost everyone will want to be as close to the route as they can get, even if they can't actually see.'

Due to growing concerns for the public's health and safety, the police did so anyway, partly to divert the crowds. With the number of incoming onlookers now estimated to be in excess of a million, police were worried about the implications of that many people clustered around a processional route that was currently too short.

As discussions continued, the obvious solution was to extend the route to allow for more space. The police commissioner suggested re-routing the procession around Trafalgar Square. He promised to look into the logistics and report back in the morning. As the meeting drew to a close we were left with the remaining questions of flags and protocols still undecided, and the delicate issue of when the Queen might address the nation still hanging frustratingly in the air.

I put it out of my mind. There was no point in doing otherwise. I had another day of broadcast arrangements with which to deal.

And for now, I just had to get some sleep.

Wednesday, 3rd September, 1997

I rose at 5am and was at the office within half an hour. My daughter, Victoria, had arrived from New York late Monday night. Nothing would have prevented her from coming, and I had told her she could take my place in the Abbey come Saturday. Regrettably, I had hardly seen her, as I had been working almost around the clock. Fuelled purely by adrenalin, I scarcely even felt tired anymore.

When I reached the Palace, I saw that there had clearly been no progress overnight with regards to the flag. The notably bare flagpole still skewered the late-summer sky. I wasn't surprised. From the start, my instinct had been that they should concede on this one point and just get the flag up there. After all, it wasn't a constitutional issue, but merely a traditional one, and sometimes traditions have to either make way for new ones or be put aside as expediency dictates.

This was such a time. Maintaining its constant pressure on the matter, the media pitted itself against equally resolute courtiers – courtiers unwilling to explain to the Queen that she was playing right into the hands of the press, thereby further fueling the negative headlines.

Part of the problem was that the media was not fully conversant with the facts. Several members were calling for the Royal Standard to be flown at half-mast, but this was never going to happen as the Royal Standard is *never* flown at half-mast. And so came the call for the Union Flag. This, too, was impossible, as the Union Flag *never* flies over Buckingham Palace...and so the debacle rumbled on.

I turned my attention to matters which were more my preserve – visiting the media encampment and having a check through of the morning papers before heading to the Chinese Dining Room for the 10am meeting.

Lord Airlie confirmed what we all already knew. There had still been no resolution on the issue of the flag, nor on two other key items for which the media was beginning to bay – that the Queen should travel down from Balmoral to be seen among her people, and that she make a televised address to the nation. The latter, were it to happen, would also be a first, as Her Majesty only addresses the nation during her annual Christmas Day message.

But this was a circumstance without precedent, and we all knew it. The nation, if not at a standstill, had certainly been gripped like never before. The Princess's death was now being discussed by media around the world, and the absence of an official royal response was becoming glaringly conspicuous.

We knew that we would have to say something within the next 24 hours. We also knew that, whatever happened next, we were at the hands of a hostile media. Had the Queen instead hurried down to London and left her grieving grandsons, she would have been attacked for being cold and uncaring. She was damned either way.

There were no more positive developments regarding the processional route either. The police commissioner had returned with the news that the proposed Trafalgar Square extension had been deemed insufficient to ease the crowd pressure, so it was back to the drawing board. But then Michael Gibbins, the Princess's Private Secretary, came up with an inspired idea.

'Why don't we take the Princess back to Kensington Palace and begin from there?' he suggested. 'We could take Her Royal Highness home for one last night on the eve of the funeral. By starting from there, we would extend the route by more than two miles.'

The police commissioner agreed at once, as did we. If workable, Michael's idea would spread the influx of people coming into London enormously, both easing the pressure on resources and giving many more people the opportunity to see the procession pass by. All we needed to do now was recce it.

That afternoon, four of us set off under the warm September sunshine to walk the route. Joining me were Lt. Col. Anthony Mather, the Assistant Comptroller in the Lord Chamberlain's office, the London District Garrison Sergeant Major, Alan 'Perry' Mason and the King's Troop CO.

The key point we needed to establish was whether the King's Troop Royal Horse Artillery's gun carriage, which would be carrying the casket, could negotiate the 90 degree turns along the way. The first hurdle was the turning circle outside the Princess's apartment, and we were all relieved to find that it was manageable. After that it was simply a matter of ticking boxes at the pillared entrance to Kensington Palace, the turning into Kensington Road, and finally the turning circle into Kensington Gardens at Queens Gate, just down the road from the Royal Albert Hall.

Having confirmed them all as untroublesome, we walked the rest of the route back to the Palace in open road. Upon our return to the office, we reported our findings to the Lord Chamberlain and the Comptroller, Lt. Colonel Malcolm Ross. All that remained now was for Lord Airlie to present the proposal to the Queen. A suggestion of this nature would normally take the form of a written note, but given the urgency, a telephone call had to suffice. Within half an hour, we had royal approval.

Given the strain already placed on their resources, I knew the latest developments would not go down brilliantly with the television networks (the BBC, ITV and SKY), but I called a priority briefing for seven o'clock that evening to break the news. The extended route was going to present a challenge, but one to which they would all have to rise.

Crammed into the office was a mixed bunch of outside broadcasters and producers, heads of events, and resources organisers – all of whom, I knew, were going to have their abilities tested to the full.

'I have good news and bad news,' I began. 'The good news is that the route I gave you on Monday is fixed. The bad news is that we have now doubled the length of it.'

Their reaction was reassuringly calm and impassive, but I knew that they were all mentally calculating whether they had the means to cover the extension. They had already stretched themselves by deciding to cover the entire route from Westminster Abbey in London to Althorp in Northamptonshire – a massive undertaking in itself. Now I had placed an added burden upon their already overextended resources.

The beginning of September, and therefore the end of the school summer holidays, is not an ideal period for an unplanned outside broadcast at the best of times. In this extraordinary situation, it was a challenge indeed, and the networks knew that they would have to pool their resources, a measure which had never been done before.

Knowing that they probably loathed the very idea of it, I left the briefing trusting that they would co-operate with each other. Camera placement was their remaining headache, now that the route had been extended. They had three days left to get everything set. I could only hope the pool would work

At the office, time was of the essence. In personal terms, it seemed non-existent. But as I worked flat out, I was ever conscious of the little voice niggling in my ear, reminding me of the person for whom I was doing all of this.

On Wednesday afternoon, I managed to find a moment to step off the treadmill and spend a brief respite reflecting on the previous few days. It had been four days since my pager had awoken me with the initial news – four of the longest and most intense days of my working life. Through it all, with the exception of the brief few hours at RAF Northholt, I had pushed all personal thoughts of Diana to the back of my mind. There really was no other way to proceed. But now that I had a little window of personal time available, I decided that I wanted to spend it with my former principal. It was 3pm when I left the office and made the short walk down the Mall to the Chapel Royal.

Located in St James's Palace, the Chapel Royal was commissioned by Henry VIII in 1531. While it might look insignificant from the outside, inside it is positively breathtaking. The Chapel contains several magnificent stained glass windows, and its ceiling was decorated in 1540 by the artist Hans Holbein, in honour of the King's short-lived fourth marriage to Anne of Cleves.

Kings and queens have been associated with the Chapel ever since. Mary Tudor's heart was buried beneath chancel step in 1558; Elizabeth I prayed there for the defense of the realm against the threat of the Spanish Armada in 1588; Charles I received Holy Communion in the Gatehouse adjoining the Chapel Royal before his execution in Whitehall in 1649 and Queen Victoria married Prince Albert there in 1840. More recently, the former Catherine Middleton was confirmed there prior to her wedding in 2011, and Prince George of Cambridge was christened amidst its hallowed walls.

In addition to the beautiful decoration and a wealth of royal history, music has long been a feature of the Chapel. Several famous composers have served as organists, including Thomas Tallis (from 1543) and Henry Purcell (from 1682). Perhaps its most famous organist was George Frideric Handel (from 1723), composer of *Zadok the Priest*, which has been sung at every coronation since the reign of George II in 1727.

The Chapel Royal is only open to the public during worship services, so on that afternoon, as with every day leading up to the funeral, it provided a place of and peace and solitude away from the public eye. It had been a trying few days, but once inside the Chapel my every emotion came to the forefront. While I had hoped for a sense of peace, it was anger that I felt most prominently upon seeing the casket resting before the altar, draped in the Royal Standard. I was angry that I should be there at all.

We all knew about the chase by the paparazzi that had led to Diana's untimely death, about how fast the car had reportedly been travelling, how Dodi Fayed had been killed on impact and how Diana had later passed away, not long after her arrival at the hospital. By extension, I also knew how different things might have been – almost certainly *would* have been – if she had just done the one thing she had always advocated – fastened her seatbelt.

I felt angry because I remembered how meticulous the Princess had always been about getting in her car and belting up. She had also always been unfailingly vocal about making sure those of us who worked for her did the same.

'Why, Ma'am?' I asked her aloud. 'Why didn't you put on your seatbelt? How could you have been so stupid?'

I was angry with the driver and her bodyguard. Why had neither of them insisted she put on her seatbelt? I knew that the events in Paris had escalated very quickly, but I still couldn't understand why no-one had pressed the point; it was such an automatic thing to do.

I must have vented my anger for at least half an hour. 'Why, Ma'am?' I kept asking over and over, feeling the rush of sorrow building inside me for such a terrible waste of a young life…and at a time when it was just becoming whole again. In hindsight I suppose my anger was just a way of bringing my own grief to the surface; I had been so wrapped up in media arrangements that I had been like an automaton since the news broke. Now, sitting in the Chapel with her, I felt all too human.

I got up and turned to leave, knowing that I would be back. There was still more I wanted to say to her, and I just wasn't ready to say goodbye.

CHAPTER 17

The Royals Return

Thursday, 4th September, 1997

I left my apartment at 5am to walk in Kensington Gardens and get my mind set for the long day ahead. It was the first time I had returned to the park since Sunday, four days prior, and I wasn't sure what to expect. While at home, I couldn't help but hear the constant buzz of people and smell the scent of flowers drifting over the wall.

I got my first look at the scene as dawn broke on another warm and windless late summer morning. There were signs that tents had been set up overnight. People continued to mill around, placing flowers on the ever-growing floral carpet. Others knelt to read the messages that were tied to bouquets or pinned onto cuddly toys. As had been the case since the day of the accident, an air of calm and peace prevailed.

No-one felt the need to hide their grief. As un-British as it seemed, men, women and children alike exhibited a comfort in sharing their emotions. I came away feeling drained and the day had only just begun.

The weather broke that day, though the scattered rain showers did little to reduce the numbers in the streets. The flowers and other tributes continued to pile up outside Kensington and Buckingham Palaces, forming drifts that would soon become outright hills.

Behind closed doors, there were more prosaic questions to be answered. With Diana's press secretary Geoff Crawford about to return from his holiday in Australia, it was time to run through the arrangements already put into place, and troubleshoot those that were not.

Aside from my having to intervene between press and police in the matter of a cherry picker, the media arrangements were all going to plan. The PR situation, however, was not.

We were under siege, and everyone knew it. Flak from the media was coming thick and fast with demands as to why no member of the Royal Family had so much as gone to pay their respects to the Princess at the Chapel Royal. Moreover, reporters were demanding to know why no-one had gone to sign the books of condolence.

The books had taken on a life all their own. We had already had to provide far more than we had initially accounted for. By Wednesday, the queues to sign them had become outlandish – the average waiting time exceeding eight hours.

This wasn't due to poor planning, but rather the fact that people seemingly weren't satisfied with merely signing the books. Having made the trip, from hundreds of miles away in many cases, and having queued for so long, they wanted to linger and take the time to write their feelings about the Princess. Had they met her personally, they often wrote about the circumstance. If not, they simply wanted to share with other mourners how Diana had impacted their lives. This was also a chance to become part of an important moment in history, so the numbers were not surprising.

In response, we produced yet more books of condolence, and soon managed to reduce wait times to a more reasonable three hours or so. Voluntary service was also drafted in to provide refreshments for those waiting.

As indeed no-one from the Royal Family had yet gone to sign the books, we were skating on thin ice from a PR standpoint. I decided to take initiative. Knowing that Prince Edward was currently staying at the Palace, and would probably be going to his office at some point, I decided to give him an early call.

'Good morning, Sir. Are you going to work today? Because if you are, I suggest that you stop off and look at the books of condolence in St James' Palace. '

'Er...I'm not sure,' he replied, doubtfully. 'I've got various things I have to do...'

This was no time for umming and ahhing. I held firm.

'I'm sorry, Sir, but we are getting a lot of flak from the media. We're fed up of being beaten up by them, frankly, and we need someone to be seen going in there.'

'Ah...but *will* anyone see me?' he asked.

At that point there were more cameras in place around the royal palaces than ever before. 'No need to worry about that,' I said. 'You will *definitely* be seen.'

I arranged to take him down there personally, after which time he could immediately return to work.

I assumed that the matter was settled, but 20 minutes later the Prince was back on the phone.

'Just to let you know, I'm not going down now, okay? I'm going with the Duke of York later on this afternoon instead.'

I mentally counted to ten, then replied, 'can we have a little chat?'

Or a big chat, if it proved necessary. It would be such a small gesture to correct such a huge negative ground-swell. How difficult could it be to understand that? I quickly primed my colleague, Penny, to be at my side when I confronted Prince Edward. I didn't need her to say anything; I just wanted her to be there.

The Prince appeared five minutes later.

'I don't understand,' I said to him. 'What exactly is the problem?'

'There's not a problem. I'm just going with the Duke of York this afternoon, that's all.'

As I couldn't very well drag him by the hand I suggested again that he should go that morning. He blinked, taken aback, but thankfully didn't argue the point. I accompanied him to St James's Palace 30 minutes later.

By day's end, Prince Edward had been to look at the books twice, once accompanied by me, and again later that afternoon alongside the Duke of York. My guess was that his reluctance had been based on fear. No-one with access to the media that week could have failed to be aware of the hostility that was brewing, and I'm sure that Prince Edward was anxious about the reaction he might receive.

I could understand this, but we simply could not afford

any reticence. No doubt Prince Andrew felt the same way as his brother. In the end, they needn't have worried. Both the waiting crowd and the press were unfailingly polite toward each of the Princes.

In readiness for the transfer of the Princess's casket to Kensington Palace from the Chapel Royal, we set a cut-off time of 6pm, on Friday 5th September, for those wishing to sign the books.

The Church House media briefing that I had set up on the Monday took place at lunchtime that Thursday, with over 600 in attendance. By now I knew that press secretary Geoff Crawford had been given the go-ahead to make a statement explaining the Queen's decision to remain at Balmoral with the rest of the family, including Princes William and Harry. While the text was being prepared, I went over to the media park at Canada Gate to ready the broadcasters for Geoff's address to camera.

Everyone was keen for the statement to go out in time for the lunchtime news bulletins. As it was still being written during ITV's 12:30 lunchtime news, it was the BBC and SKY News – whose lunchtime bulletins didn't go out until 1pm – that got the jump. ITN pressed Geoff for more information, tossing out a few questions, but Geoff stuck diligently to the text. The broadcast was a first, as no member of the Royal Household had ever made a live statement on behalf of the Palace to the press in this manner before. To my knowledge, it has not happened since.

A decision on the flag issue, with the Queen's approval, had been reached at long last. We informed the press that when Her Majesty left the Palace for the funeral service at Westminster Abbey, the Royal Standard would be replaced by the Union Flag at half-mast – a landmark occurrence.

We were also now able confirm that the Queen would return to London from Balmoral the following day, Friday, the eve of the funeral. Given the negative press coverage of late, we could only guess at the sort of welcome Her Majesty could expect upon her arrival.

It was the young Princes, then 15 and 12, who first had to face the scrutiny of the watching world. They arrived back in London that afternoon. Along with their father, they paid a visit to Kensington Palace, seeing in person for the first time the blanket of flowers covering the area, and speaking with a number of the gathered mourners.

There is a royal adage of unknown origin that reads: *You don't wear private grief on a public sleeve.* In my many years of working for 'the firm', I had seen it put into practice on many occasions, but perhaps never so poignantly as on that afternoon. Watching the spontaneous walkabout on the television in the Buckingham Palace press office, I could only marvel at the composure displayed by William and Harry, even as all around them the public wept and wailed.

While such a demonstration of integrity indicated that they would be strong enough to make the long walk expected of them come Saturday, it also served as a sobering reminder that in the midst of this global event, there were two bereft and broken-hearted boys.

Friday, 5th September, 1997

The day began with what would be the last Lord Chamberlain's meeting. With little more than 24 hours left before the funeral, there was still a great deal to be done logistically, and the imminent arrival of Her Majesty and the Duke of Edinburgh meant a whole new set of additional concerns.

Initial considerations involved the short walkabout they would be undertaking (to St James's Palace to look at the books of condolence), as well as their return by royal car to Buckingham Palace, where they would view the mountain of flowers that had collected outside the gates and meet a few of those who had come to pay their respects.

It was a trying time for the broadcasters. Having commandeered additional equipment and personnel from all regions, they were now struggling for position along the extended route, all the while fearful of missing their deadline. For me, this meant a great deal of trouble-shooting and responding to an endless stream of queries, requests and snags. I sent countless faxes; my mobile phone scarcely left my ear and my pager was like a small jittery animal in my pocket.

Understandably, it was a day of quibbles. As the cameramen jockeyed for position, owners and tenants of private apartments along the route wanted confirmation from the press office that the arriving broadcasters were authorized.

We had already scaled back the number of cameras that would be allowed inside the Abbey, conscious that every family had a right to attend a loved one's funeral without the intrusion of long lenses capturing its grief. But the privacy issue extended outside the Abbey as well. The Royal Parks, which was against allowing broadcast vehicles into Hyde Park, maintained that the post-Abbey drive should be private. I argued that an open drive through the streets of London could hardly be deemed private in any sense.

With some reluctance, DCMS and Royal Parks stood down, agreeing to allow broadcast vehicles into Hyde Park to ensure uninterrupted television coverage.

The Queen was scheduled to go on television at 6pm to deliver her personal tribute to the Princess. The BBC was selected as the pool broadcaster for the address and immediately narrowed the possible locations down to two – the Belgian Suite or the Centre Room.

To my mind, both suggestions were non-starters. Geoff and I had already decided the broadcast should go out from the Chinese Dining Room, with the French doors open and the public activity beyond serving as a backdrop.

The BBC's Philip Gilbert initially resisted our recommendation, citing concerns of the ambient noise, but he eventually came around and accepted that it was the perfect setting.

Her Majesty's televised tribute would be another royal first, as she had never addressed the nation in this manner before. None of us doubted for a moment that she would perform flawlessly.

Neither the Queen nor the Duke of Edinburgh blamed one party over the other for the collapse of the Waleses marriage. They believed both Charles and Diana were equally at fault.

They were especially saddened by the demise as, contrary to popular belief, they were both very fond of Diana. In her public address on the eve of the funeral, the Queen expressed her depth of feeling when she spoke from the heart saying:

'She was an exceptional and gifted human being. In good times and in bad, she never lost her capacity to smile and laugh, nor inspire others with her warmth and kindness. I admired and respected her for her energy and commitment to others, and especially for her devotion to her two boys. I share in your determination to cherish her memory.'

Amidst all of the day's madness, I made sure to find time to attend to some unfinished business from earlier in the week.

Professionally, the Princess had obviously been on my mind throughout, but I had risen that morning thinking of her on a personal level as well.

I walked over to the Chapel Royal and found to my good fortune that there wasn't anyone around.

The anger I had felt on my previous visit had left me. As I stood beside the casket for the second time, my fingertips lightly resting on the fabric of the Royal Standard, I felt nothing but warmth and affection for the woman I had known. I talked to her about the good times we'd had over the years – my wonderful 50th Birthday lunch, all the Royal tours, the jokes and silly games.

I thought about the times she wouldn't speak to me for a couple of weeks because I'd negated one of her suggestions, how she would later phone me for a favor only to hear me say, 'Are we talking again, then?'

She would giggle, and just like that I would be back at her bidding.

In the quiet of the Chapel Royal, I thanked her for being so incredibly kind to my daughter, both in person and once she had left to begin her studies in the USA. I thanked her for the notes she'd written to Victoria from time to time, asking how she was getting on.

I admitted that I'd given Victoria my ticket to the funeral, stating that, as ever, I'd be tied up in the press office, mobile phone in hand, troubleshooting.

'Would that be alright, Ma'am?' I asked her. 'I hope you don't mind.'

Something told me she would probably approve.

I don't know how long I spent with her, certainly not more than 40 minutes. What I do know is that when I was done, I had talked myself out. I placed a hand fully atop the casket and rested it there a moment in a final farewell.

'Goodbye Ma'am...and thank you.'

I bowed from the neck, and left the Chapel.

Not being able to count on how the public would react, anxieties intensified as we anticipated the arrival back in London of the Queen and the Duke of Edinburgh.

The Mall is normally closed to traffic on Sundays, and early on the day of the Princess's death, the Royal Parks Police had already made the decision that it would remain closed for the duration of the week, culminating with the funeral. It was now beginning to fill up with people, another cause for concern.

Crowds had been milling about Buckingham Palace, The Mall and St James's Palace all week, but now there was a sense that they were no longer returning home. There were even signs that some intended to camp out all night in order to secure a prime spot along the processional route.

In the short term, however, many of those hardened individuals would have a chance at an up-close view of their sovereign. We could only hope that they would remain friendly.

The Queen and the Duke of Edinburgh had left Buckingham Palace for the Chapel Royal by mid-afternoon. The plan was that they would pay their respects to Diana, and then proceed through the Long Corridor at St James's Palace to meet with members of the public signing the condolence books. There would then be a short walkabout along Marlborough Road to The Mall, and finally the brief drive to Buckingham Palace.

I arrived at St James's Palace ahead of the Queen and Prince Philip in order to be on hand if needed. I knew the next hour would perhaps be one of Her Majesty's most difficult, given the element of public anger in recent days, partially induced by the media.

We in the press office believed that the situation could have been helped enormously if only the flag issue had been addressed sooner, and if there had at least been some sort of public confirmation that Her Majesty would be paying tribute to the Princess on the eve of the funeral.

Our only hope was that the next 20 hours or so would provide a platform whereby we could repair some of the damage. Whatever the rights or wrongs of the situation, Her Majesty had to go out in public and face a potentially antagonistic crowd, and so at the moment, my concern was solely focused on my boss.

I arrived at St James's Palace to find that the police seemed to share my concerns, although I felt they had somewhat overreacted. I saw no way for the Queen and Duke of Edinburgh to interact with the public from behind the wall of uniformed policemen and policewomen that had been put in place.

While Her Majesty and the Duke were inside the Chapel Royal, I went and spoke to the senior officer. He agreed that their numbers were over the top, and many of the police personnel were withdrawn.

The couple eventually emerged and spent 20 minutes completing the short walk from St James's Palace to The Mall (a distance of no more than 160 feet), as they spoke with people who'd come to pay their respects.

So far, all was going to plan. I had stood alongside Her Majesty throughout the walk, with the Duke of Edinburgh, as usual, a few paces behind. I was relieved that the Queen had been mostly met with smiles and respectfully muted applause.

Once she and the Duke had got back into the royal car, I jumped inside the police back-up vehicle so that I could meet up with them once again at Buckingham Palace.

The car stopped just inside the North Centre Gate. Her Majesty stepped out to a ripple of polite applause from the large crowd. We had already set up barriers, so that the Queen and Prince Philip could view the floral tributes and again speak to the mourners.

I hurried across to join them, briefing the Queen as we walked, letting her know what had been happening in her absence, and informing her that the flowers had begun to appear at the railings as early as five o'clock on the morning of the Princess's death.

Her Majesty and the Duke moved easily before the crowd, talking to individuals and listening to their words of condolence. At one point the Queen offered to place some flowers atop the drift of bouquets for an 11-year-old girl only to be told, 'No Your Majesty...these are for *you.*' I was happy to see Her Majesty on the receiving end of such a warm gesture.

Clearly the media had not read all the signs correctly. Contrary to reports, the great British public wasn't as hostile towards the Monarchy as we'd been made to believe.

It is my belief that people had finally taken time to think about why the Queen had chosen to remain at Balmoral. Perhaps they'd also taken into consideration what the young Princes had been able to do the previous afternoon. There was no doubt in my mind that those boys had been able to steel themselves for the task at hand largely because of that crucial time spent with their grand-parents, away from public scrutiny.

As we neared the car, the Queen turned to me and we had a brief conversation about her appearance outside the gates of Buckingham Palace. I had been in her proximity for a good number of years by this stage, so it would have taken a lot for her to surprise me … and yet our small conversation did. My response was straightforward: 'That was fine, Your Majesty, Just fine.' I bowed from the neck and she disappeared into the car.

I returned to my office with the Queen's words still ringing in my ears, but I kept them to myself. That I had been inspired by my boss of nine years went without saying, but at that moment I was reminded of just how inspirational a person the Queen is. Yes, one can dwell on the twin buzzwords of wealth and privilege, but it seems to me that to do so is to draw attention away from another word – duty.

With the unfailing support of her husband, she continues to perform her duties in service to her country with meritable grace, living by her mother's mantra: *Never complain, never explain.*

That day in particular she exhibited a remarkable sense of self that seemed to insulate her from the slingshots aimed at her, at members of her family and at the institution of Monarchy itself.

That the Queen had said those few words to me spoke volumes, and realizing that she had sought my support, however small, moved me greatly. I will never forget it, and I was glad to have been able to reassure her...because it *was* fine.

CHAPTER 18

Farewell to the People's Princess

With the soft afternoon sunshine falling on the crowds milling below, and the rumble of quiet conversation setting exactly the right scene, the Queen's live tribute to Diana went out at 6pm as planned. Her Majesty spoke fluently and eloquently, and as we watched, along with the rest of the nation, we all heaved a mental sigh of relief. The Sovereign had spoken to her people, and all was as it should be.

With everything else in place that evening, we needed only to transfer the Princess from the Chapel Royal to Kensington Palace. It had been decided that the casket should be placed in a quiet vestibule between the entrance hall and the stairwell, where Reverend Willie Booth, sub-dean of the Chapel Royal and the only full-time member of the Queen's ecclesiastical household, was going to keep an all-night vigil with the Princess.

Prior to that, however, the casket had to be transported.

The police were keen to keep the exact departure time a secret. They had decided not to erect crash barriers, believing that to do so would only encourage more spectators, not to mention involve a great deal of extra manpower and disruption to traffic. Instead they opted to rely on their Special Escort Group to oversee the transfer. It would be impossible to keep the move completely under wraps; the media had already been told that the gun carriage would be departing for the Abbey the following morning from Kensington Palace rather than the Chapel Royal, but the goal was to cause as minimal disruption as possible.

With such a large media presence in the area, and an unparalleled number of cameras already in position, there was never going to be much chance of making the final move to Kensington Palace without it being carried live across all the UK and global news networks.

The broadcasters were duly diligent. They had kept a steady watch on St James's Palace, so as the great doors swung open and the hearse appeared, the cameras were rolling to document Diana's journey to spend a final night in the apartment that she had called home since 1981.

The police effort to keep the move as covert an operation as possible proved futile. Having expected the transfer, thousands of spectators lined the route from Piccadilly to the entrance of Kensington Palace Avenue to silently pay their respects as the hearse made its slow progress to the Princess's home – a journey of just over two miles. The only other expression of public sentiment that evening was the occasional single flower thrown in the path of the hearse.

In terms of professional responsibilities, my day was almost done. Once the Princess's casket had arrived inside Kensington Palace, I made a final pass around all of the broadcasters to check that nobody had any last minute glitches and to let them know that my pager would be beside me if they had any emergencies, whatever the hour. The following day would see a broadcast event the likes of which had never been witnessed before, and given the limited amount of time we'd had to organise and stage it, it seemed almost impossible that it could go without a hitch.

With my former principal resting just across the private lawn, I felt a sense of calm overtake me as I climbed into bed. My pager remained silent throughout the night.

Saturday, 6th September, 1997

The morning of the funeral dawned dry and warm, with the sun rising into clear blue skies. It was going to be another hot day. Roads were closed off early in order to give the police time to canvas the route, and as I had made a conscious decision to leave my car at home, I made my way to Kensington High Street underground station around 6am, to catch an already crowded tube to Victoria.

From there it was just a short walk to Buckingham Palace, and an early start to what I knew would be a very long day. I arrived at 6:30am, determined to be ahead of the game and pre-empt any potential problems. I went straight to the media camp behind Canada Gate to ensure that all was well with the various broadcasters, who were already on air. Like the rest of us, they knew that today of all days there was no room for error. Apart from one minor panic over a pool camera that the police suddenly wanted resituated, all was calm and orderly as the clock ticked towards 9:08am – the time at which Diana, Princess of Wales would begin the first part of her final journey.

I don't think anyone who was there, or who watched the coverage on television, will forget the poignancy and intensity of what they witnessed that morning: the mournful clang of the Abbey bell reverberating across London as it marked each sorrowful minute of the Princess's journey to Westminster Abbey, the sound of the gun carriage's wheels, the clip-clop of the horses' hooves, the click of hobnail boots striking the tarred road as the cortege wended its slow and solemn way through the streets. Nor will they forget the sight of the Royal Standard-draped casket, topped with three all-white wreaths of lilies, roses and tulips from the Spencer family. Also atop the casket was perhaps the most moving televisual sight of the day – the wreath from William and Harry. Placed on it was a card that would set the emotional tone for the rest of the coverage. It simply – and so very sadly – read *Mummy*.

Like millions of others, my colleagues and I in the press office watched the procession on television. I stayed until 10:10am, then walked out of Buckingham Palace's North Centre Gates, as the Queen and other members of the Royal Family left through the Privy Purse door, bound for the North Gate, where they would wait for the gun carriage to pass before making their way to the Abbey.

As I took up my own position by the North Centre

Gates, I saw something I had never seen before. Someone had tied a huge banner to the Palace railings, which simply proclaimed 'Diana of Love'. It seemed to sum up the moment, the day and the public sentiment. There was no question of anyone removing it.

As the cortege drew level, my gaze happened to be on the Queen, whom I saw respectfully bow her head as it passed. I hoped the cameras had caught the symbolic gesture. The air hung with sadness. There was scarcely a sound save for that which came from the cortege itself, the occasional sob from an overcome member of the public, and the tolling of the minute-bell from Westminster Abbey. Even the birds had stopped singing, as if they too understood that Saturday, 6th September 1997 was a solemn day.

Suddenly, hidden somewhere within the throngs of spectators, a lone piper began to play. The song was 'Flowers of the Forest', a haunting Scottish folk tune, which is only ever played at funerals and memorial services. It is a piece that invariably sends shivers down my spine, and nevermore so as on that day. Like the tens of thousands around me, I had to fight to hold back tears.

Halfway down The Mall, at its junction with Marlborough Road, the five male members of the family awaited the cortege in order to walk behind it for the remainder of the journey to Westminster Abbey. The Prince of Wales stood with his brow deeply furrowed. Next to him, pale and struggling to come to terms with the day, was his youngest son, Prince Harry. Earl Spencer, head bowed in respect, reached out his left hand to support his nephew. To his right, his other nephew, Prince William, also stood with head lowered in readiness for the coming ordeal. Flanking William was his grandfather, Prince Philip.

As the gun carriage came abreast of the walking male members of the family, the four royal princes bowed their heads. Diana's brother looked straight ahead and crossed himself. They then joined the cortege, lining up behind the gun carriage, the five of them now principal mourners ahead of the 500 representing the Princess's charities.

Watching the men and boys take their place, there was no question in my mind that the Duke of Edinburgh was central to their standing there. Indeed, if it hadn't been for the love and support of both their grandparents, I wonder if the young Princes would have been able to find the strength to take part in such a public – and some might argue – intrusive part of the ceremony. Yet they did, with the eyes and ears of the world following their every move. At times, it was almost too difficult to watch, but I know their mother would have been extremely proud.

There has never been a funeral like that of Diana, Princess of Wales. There were in excess of a million people lining the cortege route from Kensington Palace to Westminster Abbey, and then on to Althorp. The giant screen in Hyde Park allowed for more than 100,000 people to watch the events unfold, and loudspeakers placed along the route offered spectators the opportunity to hear – and participate with – the service.

The proceedings went out live, and were beamed worldwide to an audience estimated at 2.5 billion people speaking 44 languages in 200 countries. In the UK alone, the television audience numbered an unprecedented 33 million.

Depending on your viewpoint, there were also tensions that day. At the time of her death, the Princess's relationship with her brother had noticeably cooled. It wasn't for us to speculate about the details, but it was later widely reported that there were disagreements about the Althorp Estate between the Princess and her brother, and with nowhere to go other than her apartment at Kensington Palace, the Princess was very aggrieved by this.

No reference to this was evident on this day, however. On the contrary, Earl Spencer made a scathing – and now famous – verbal attack on both the media and, very pointedly, the Royal Family, in his address during the funeral service.

Paying tribute to the sister with whom he had so recently been at odds in life, he now called Diana 'a symbol of selfless humanity' and a 'standard bearer of the rights of the downtrodden.' He went on to add that, 'she needed no royal title to generate her brand of magic' – a clear reference to the withdrawal of her title 'Her Royal Highness' at the time of her divorce from the Prince of Wales the previous year.

The impassioned speech elicited a ripple of applause among the crowds listening outside the Abbey, which soon increased in volume and intensity. Before long it could be heard far and wide, not least by the congregation inside the Abbey. The majority of us watching and listening in the press office were appalled. Personally,

I felt the speech had been outrageous. Yes, by all means grieve; certainly feel aggrieved at the manner and timing of your sister's death. That would be perfectly under-standable. But to do so in a church, at a solemn service, felt unforgiveable on many fronts. It was neither the time nor the place for such action, especially given that Diana's children were present.

The Princess was placed in a hearse for the journey to her childhood home at Althorp and followed by a suite car carrying the deputy comptroller of the Lord Chamberlain's Office. Although the entire route had been officially closed to traffic, the police needn't have bothered. No-one was driving anywhere that day. At Hyde Park Corner, seven black-clad Special Escort Group (SEG) police motorcyclists took up their positions to guide the hearse on its long drive – three in 'V' formation in the front, and two either side of the hearse.

Tens of thousands of people lined the route as the sad cavalcade made its slow progress through the streets of London, north to the M1, and on to Althorp, for a private interment on a small island in the middle of the lake there. It was a distance of 77 miles, but onlookers flanked every possible inch of it, many of them throwing flowers towards the vehicle. Due to the disruption that throngs of visitors would likely cause, the family had decided against interring Diana in the family vault at Great Brington.

Along with my colleagues, I watched the trip in its entirety on television in the Buckingham Palace press office, ready to deal with any problem that might require our intervention. I was struck by how the driver had to keep using his windscreen wipers to clear away the flowers. If there had been any doubt in life, it was very apparent in death, that the British public was united in its love for Diana.

I marveled at the outpouring of love and respect, and hoped the Princes would draw comfort from the great show of support from every direction. As she had hoped, she truly had become the 'Queen of People's Hearts'. I'd also like to believe that it was their way of making sure she wasn't alone for her passage home.

Althorp's wrought-iron gates closed behind Diana at 5:30pm that Saturday afternoon, thus ending the journey to her final resting place. The irony of the location wasn't lost on me. The place she had so desperately wanted to call home while alive was now hers in death.

My own day, which for all practical purposes had begun a whole week earlier, on August 31st, was now done.

Many people had strong opinions about Diana, Princess of Wales. I don't doubt there are many who still do. But as someone who knew her well, the one tag I never really felt summed her up as a person, was that which the Prime Minister Tony Blair gave her – the 'People's Princess.' Yes, she was the Princess in people's hearts that she had always aspired to be. But at the same time, she was very much her own person. She was a one-off, and however many column inches are written about her, history will decide how she should be remembered.

I felt deeply saddened by her death, but I knew we had served her well. The team at Buckingham Palace, the private secretary's office, the Lord Chamberlain's office and the press office, achieved in six days what many had thought might well be impossible, and we did it with the dignity and precision that one expects from the Palace. I was proud to have been part of that team.

I had known Diana for 17 years, first as a young woman in her late teens bursting onto centre stage in 1980, then as a fully-fledged member of the Royal Family, doing her share of duties with professionalism and flair.

I had reported her movements for eight years as Court Correspondent for IRN, and then handled her media-related affairs at Buckingham Palace.

During her 16 years as a member of the Royal Family, she undertook some wonderful work, putting a definitive lid on the myths surrounding diseases like leprosy and AIDS, as well as drawing attention to those who had been so often overlooked – the homeless, drug and alcohol addicts, the victims of land mines and so many others for whom life had dealt a hard blow.

She was a full-time mother, who cherished and nurtured her sons, and she flew the flag for independent women everywhere.

I travelled a great deal with her, on solo visits to the USA, Egypt and Pakistan, as well as on many worldwide joint visits with the Prince of Wales. We spent countless hours in each other's company, aboard planes and in hotels. We had enjoyed many laughs, and we had the occasional differences of opinion.

In the five years I looked after her and Charles, she

frustrated me more than once, but the good times far outweighed the bad.

Though we were all subjected to a freeze every now and then, most of us made it back. I was lucky in doing so, and even when I stopped looking after her, we had regular contact either by phone, correspondence or when passing one another on foot or in the car, always stopping for a chat.

Diana, Princess of Wales left this earth too soon. I was deeply shocked when I heard the news of the crash and devastated over her death. I don't think I even quite believed it until I saw her coffin gently removed from the aircraft at RAF Northolt. I did have a very soft spot for her, and yes, I was very fond of her. As I told her, I would miss her. I still do.

CHAPTER 19

All Quiet on the SW1 Front

The days immediately following Diana's funeral were anticlimactic in the extreme. Working flat-out for seven straight days had rendered everyone physically, mentally and emotionally exhausted. That is not to say that there wasn't a sense of satisfaction in knowing that when given a seemingly insurmountable project, we had risen to the occasion. The media consistently accused Palace courtiers of being out of touch, but we had demonstrated that with matters of ceremony we were distinctly in touch.

It was also a time of much discussion regarding personnel around the office, and the funeral proved to be a catalyst for a fairly radical staff change. I have always believed that the Buckingham Palace press office, though extremely professional, has an unenviable and sometimes impossible job spec to fulfill.

It wasn't always that way. Prior to the engagement of Prince Charles and Lady Diana Spencer in 1981, the British press showed little appetite for the salacious trials and tribulations of a royal marriage. I'm not sure if this was down to a natural deference to the aristocracy – something deeply ingrained in the British psyche – or rather a lack of prurient interest, but our press certainly wasn't cut from the same cloth as that of our French counterparts.

According to early dispatches from France, the Queen had more than her fair share of media-driven *Annus Horribilis*. In the first 15 years of her reign alone, the French press was kept extremely busy commenting upon 73 reports that she and Prince Philip were to divorce, 63 forecasts of her imminent abdication and a whopping 92 revelations that she was pregnant.

In contrast, our domestic media was extremely reticent for a time. But then, as the trend for both divorce and public soul-baring began to steadily rise, so too did the interest in royal affairs of the heart. Gradually the public started to lean towards topics of a more personal nature than the matters of state which had led before.

In turn, it meant the press office had a rather more complex and thankless task at hand than ever before. From the early days of the Prince and Princess of Wales's relationship, to that of the Duke and Duchess of York five years later, the press office was constantly put into the difficult position of being reactive rather than pro-active, particularly when it came to the private lives of its various principals.

Stories about what the young royals were up to in their private time were invariably splashed, without our prior knowledge, across the front pages of the tabloids. It wasn't helpful when friends of Prince Charles talked openly and critically about the Princess, or when the Princess talked directly to the media. Things only went from bad to worse when the Duchess of York, still very much married to Prince Andrew at the time, latched on to Texan oil man, Steve Wyatt, and then to financial advisor, Johnny Bryan. No matter what we said or did in response to the sensational stories these liaisons generated, we were fighting a losing battle.

Even those closest to 'The Firm' couldn't always be relied upon to offer the best guidance for fear of how it would be received by the royal in question. The media frenzy over flags and flagpoles that ensued following Diana's death was a perfect case in point. Although we dealt quite ably with the issue of Her Majesty remaining with her grandsons at Balmoral, we were thrown to the wolves when it came to that glaringly bare flagpole, despite our protestations that the Union Flag should be flown at half-mast.

It wasn't a case of the press office not doing its job on the public relations front, but rather a case of common-sense advice being ignored further up the chain of command. The media debacle surrounding the funeral and subsequent public backlash led to a somewhat knee-jerk reaction from the Palace in terms of communications, so much so that when the dust settled a plan was devised to bring in a Communications Secretary. The role of this hypothetical employee was to oversee the press office, draw up strategies and deal with crisis management, which was tantamount to saying that the press secretaries were incapable of carrying out these duties themselves. Not only were we conducting our roles effectively, but we were also overseeing the British Monarchy's newly-launched website, which went live in March of 1997. Suffice to say, the suggestion that an outside PR expert was necessary did not go down well.

That the modern age required a press office capable of undertaking radical change wasn't in doubt, but it already had an established personnel which was more than capable of meeting those challenges. The hiring of a Communications Secretary led to a contentious couple of years filled with opposition and resentment.

From a personal standpoint, my final two years working for the Royal Family were relatively uneventful. During my tenure I had weathered many a tumultuous storm, but now, in my twilight years at the Palace, I had perhaps the most enviable job of all – overseeing press relations for Her Majesty the Queen. Suddenly, my working life felt calm. Our Monarch is loved for good reason, and press-managing her relationship with her people was never less than a joy.

I had thoroughly enjoyed every aspect of my role with the Royal Collection. I don't believe anyone can tire of Windsor Castle. It doesn't matter how many times one goes there, there is always something new to see.

I had been fortunate enough to attend several State Banquets at the Castle, each time seated at a magnificently laid 120-foot table in St George's Hall. Prior to any such occasion the Queen would always inspect the room to ensure that everything was just right, from the seating arrangements and table settings to the microphone neatly concealed amidst the floral arrangement opposite her seat.

In October 1997, I received an invitation to attend a ball at the Castle to be held the following month in celebration of the Queen and the Duke of Edinburgh's Golden Wedding Anniversary. I had been given no indication as to how the guest list of 300 had been compiled, but I knew that it would include every member of the Royal Family, friends and senior members of the Household.

We arrived at the Castle at the appointed time of 10:15pm and made our way up the grand staircase towards the State Apartments, assuming that we would then be directed to either the Waterloo Chamber, the Grand Reception Room or St George's Hall. Upon reaching the top of the stairs we were greeted by the Queen and Prince Philip, who were in place to welcome each of their guests with a handshake and a few words.

The band in full swing, it was clear that the Waterloo Chamber was strictly for dancing. The Grand Reception Room had been designated for socializing, and St Georges Hall – the largest room in the Castle at 180-feet long – had been arranged with round tables and chairs, and a half-bar with canapés at one end.

I had walked through St George's Hall a number of times during the restoration, and yet I still marveled at the level of skill and craftsmanship that had gone into restoring it to its former glory. It was beautiful.

We were halfway down the Hall when I turned to my wife, Rosemary, and said, 'There's four of a kind over there.'

'What are you talking about?' she replied.

'Only in Windsor Castle…four genuine queens,' I said.

As other guests mingled around them, Queen Margrethe of Denmark, Queen Beatrix of Holland, Queen Sofia of Spain and Queen Anne-Marie of Greece sat chatting amiably.

I continued to show Rosemary around the newly-restored areas, and when we reached the end of the Hall we entered the Lantern Lobby, which had previously been the private chapel. Five years earlier it had been the site where the initial fire started; now it served as an open space providing a thoroughfare between the State Apartments and the Queen's private apartments. Princess Anne was there waxing lyrical on the restoration project to a group of guests, though her information wasn't entirely correct. She caught my eye and the slight shake of my head, to which she said, 'Thank you, Dickie,' before moving on.

It was a grand ball, allowing for a once in a lifetime experience. A 60th wedding anniversary ball held in a newly-restored Windsor Castle – I don't believe I have ever seen the Queen so happy.

In 1998, Mary Francis, one of the Queen's private secretaries, suggested a 'themed away-day' for the Queen and the Duke of Edinburgh. It was a concept that proved to be a breakthrough in terms of the perceived formality of royal visits. Their first such away-day fell during the spring of 1998, and was aimed specifically at London's theatre industry. It provided the perfect opportunity to showcase homegrown talent.

In the morning, the Queen went to see youngsters put through their paces at the National Theatre on the South

Bank before going on to visit the Lyceum Theatre, where a rehearsal of *Oklahoma!* was in progress. Meanwhile, Prince Philip made a trip to the Adelphi Theatre in the Strand to watch a rehearsal of *Chicago*.

I don't think I could be accused of betraying any confidences by saying that the choice of show was probably right up Prince Philip's alley given the cast of ladies dressed in leotards and fishnets. Later that morning he rejoined the Queen to take a look around Angels, the famous theatre and film costumiers in the heart of London's West End.

Established in 1840, Angels is legendary. To date, the company has won 32 Academy Awards for Best Costume Design for its work on films such as *Titanic, The Great Gatsby* and *Lawrence of Arabia*. Both the Queen and Prince Philip were fascinated by what they a saw, and would have spent longer looking around were it not for a pressing lunch engagement at The Ivy.

The afternoon continued with a visit to one of Britain's most prestigious drama schools, The Royal Academy of Dramatic Art (RADA), before the royal couple returned to the Palace to prepare for the evening performance of *Oklahoma!* back at the Lyceum Theatre. *Oklahoma!* was the first musical the Queen ever saw in 1947, and knowing her taste in music, I managed to persuade her private secretary to include it in the day's programme of events.

The audience wasn't told that there would be royalty in the house that evening, nor was a distinctive red and gold royal box organised. The first inkling that anyone had of the Queen and Prince Philip's arrival was when they appeared at the entrance to the royal circle. Upon seeing them the audience leapt to its feet, alerting those in the stalls below to an unannounced arrival. By the time the couple had reached their seats, the theatre had erupted into spontaneous applause.

My fondest memory of that day was seeing the Queen, her feet tap-tap-tapping to the music…just another member of the public enjoying a great night out.

Having gone down so well, we decided that the 'away-day' should become a permanent fixture on the calendar for both the Queen and the Duke of Edinburgh. The first such day had been a tremendous success, and so we quickly planned another, this time to Liverpool. The day was themed around the 'built environment', focusing mainly on inner-city regeneration and ending with a visit to the newly-refurbished Empire Theatre, to see *The Phantom of the Opera*.

Having seen how well the public responded when Her Majesty and the Duke of Edinburgh arrived unannounced for the performance of *Oklahoma!*, we had really got the bit between our teeth. The Empire's theatre management asked if the Queen would unveil a commemorative plaque following the performance. Given that there would be an audience present, I suggested that we do things slightly differently in order that they, too, be allowed to share in the occasion.

Usually, when the Queen undertakes unveilings of this kind she draws a curtain in front of a plaque set into the foyer wall of whichever building or place is involved. On this occasion, however, I thought that with us being in a theatre, it might be more fun to do the unveiling on stage. I also thought that we should keep it as a surprise for the audience. Private Secretary, Mary Francis, was slightly hesitant at first, but I assured her that Her Majesty would be more than happy to go along with the plan.

According to the protocol set for when royalty is present, the audience was asked to stay in its seats while the Queen and Prince Philip went backstage to meet the cast. Minutes later, as opposed to hearing an announcement that they were free to leave the theatre, the curtain rose to reveal Her Majesty unveiling the plaque on stage.

The audience's response was extremely gratifying. It is perhaps easy to underestimate the thrill of heading off to the theatre only to find oneself unexpectedly in the company of royalty. The applause and cheering was thunderous; it was as if the Queen was having her very own curtain call.

Meanwhile, there was another couple waiting in the wings for its moment in the spotlight – Prince Charles and Mrs Camilla Parker Bowles.

It had been over a year since Diana had died, and more than six years had passed since her formal separation from Charles. In turn, Camilla and her ex-husband, Andrew, had finalized their divorce in 1995. But if the tabloids were to be believed, there were still pockets of resistance to the idea of the Prince being seen in public with Camilla. The idea had been the topic of much discussion in Prince Charles's office at St James's Palace. It was decided that the least obtrusive way of going about it would be with a carefully orchestrated publicity stunt.

The Prince of Wales and Camilla Parker Bowles made their first combined public appearance at the Ritz Hotel in London on Friday, 29th January, 1999 at a 50th birthday party for Camilla's sister, Annabel Elliott. As it was not an official engagement, the press were not briefed in advance. And yet how did so many photographers and reporters just so happen to be in the right place at the right time that night?

They had been given an old-fashioned tip-off in the form of a phone call from the St James's Palace Communications Secretary. In giving a tip-off, the hope was that the subsequent TV and print coverage would do the job of making the couple official, without the need for a formal announcement.

As stunts go it turned out to be a roaring success. The Prince emerged from the hotel first, closely followed by Camilla, which was the cue to get the cameras whirring and flashes popping. There had not been a commotion like it since the days of Diana. An estimated 200 photographers descended on the entrance to the hotel just off London's Piccadilly, with 60 ladders lined up three rows deep, television satellite vans parked in several side streets and bright television lights illuminating the whole scene.

Alongside the media, several hundred members of the public waited to catch a glimpse as well. Such was the ferocity of the flashguns that evening that newscasters were prompted to warn onlookers who suffered from photosensitive seizures to move away.

As Charles and Camilla walked down the steps of the Ritz towards their a waiting car, there was a cacophony of shouts and whoops, the mood of the evening being summed up by a woman in the crowd whom, to our delight – and surely to that of the Prince – waved and shouted, 'Good on you, Charlie!'

It was indeed good to see Prince Charles in a happy place at last, but the dawning of a new era for him on a personal level also served as a reminder that my spell at the Palace was winding down all too quickly. When I joined Buckingham Palace on 1st July, 1988, I knew from the outset that come midnight on 24th September, 2000, I would be required to retire. Suddenly the day I had dreaded was looming just over the horizon.

CHAPTER 20

Come back, Dickie – we need you!

March 2001

I left my job at the Palace in September 2000, and our cosy apartment at Kensington Palace a few weeks later. It was an emotional time but, having been acutely aware of my rapidly approaching retirement date, I had readied myself for the change and was excited for my next chapter.

Upon retiring, I promptly secured a year-long contract with the BBC to act as a freelance royal commentator, which meant being on call and available whenever a royal story broke. Having brushed up on my rusty ice dancing skills, I had also signed up to do an ice skating teaching course, something which, as it turns out, had not gone unnoticed. Just before I left the Palace, *The Times's* Picture Desk presented me with an appropriate keepsake – a composite picture of Olympic ice dancing gold medalists, Jayne Torvill and Christopher Dean, but with my and Her Majesty's heads superimposed.

When I had my farewell audience with the Queen in

the 1855 Room a couple of weeks after leaving the press office, I took the photo with me.

'What have you got there?' asked the Equerry, Squadron Leader Simon Brailsford, eyeing my envelope suspiciously. I was waiting in the adjoining Bow Room to be ushered in when I opened my envelope and slipped out the picture for him to see. He gasped.

'You can't show Her Majesty that!'

I grinned. 'Oh, trust me I can,' I said. 'And I fully intend to.'

And I had the perfect opportunity to do so.

After thanking me for my service and presenting me with my leaving gift, the Queen asked, 'what are you going to do next?'

I told her I was returning to the other side of the fence to work as a freelance royal commentator. 'But I'm also going to do some skating, and as patron of the National Ice Skating Association, which you are, I thought you might like to have a look at this, Ma'am.'

While the Queen fetched her reading glasses, I pulled out the picture. Upon seeing it she responded exactly as I had expected. She smiled broadly. The Queen is bestowed with many traits, but what people often don't know is that she has an excellent sense of humor.

Though my tenure in the press office was formally over, I received a call from my former colleague, Penny Russell-Smith, the following March, asking if I would consider returning to the Palace for a couple of weeks, as they were apparently short of an experienced pair of hands.

COME BACK, DICKIE — WE NEED YOU!

I arrived a few days later, expecting nothing more taxing than a couple of weeks reacquainting myself with some former colleagues and perhaps a chance for a nostalgic swim in the Buckingham Palace pool, but that didn't prove to be the case.

I had barely returned when we were pressed into urgent action. A news story was about to break, one that would need prompt and decisive action to contain it. It involved a royal couple with whom I had previously not had a great deal to do with, namely Prince Edward and his wife Sophie, Countess of Wessex.

When Prince Edward married Sophie Rhys-Jones in June 1999, he was still producing documentaries for his television company Ardent Productions, and Sophie continued to work in the PR industry. She was still doing so at this time, and it was while engaged in a project that she fell victim to a fake sheikh sting set up by the now defunct *News of the World*.

News of the World stories tended to rear their ugly heads on a Friday afternoon at 5pm on the dot. This was so common one really could set one's watch by them. But this was the era of the new communications secretary, who managed things differently. The journalist involved was offered an exclusive interview along with a picture of Sophie Wessex in exchange for the paper dropping the story.

In my view the correct course of action would have been to put out a spoiler to all the other newspapers, essentially giving the competition information relating to the story, which would mean the paper with the 'exclusive' no longer had an exclusive. By countering in this way, salacious stories were promptly diffused, and the whole debacle would be over within a relatively painless 24 hours.

Sadly, that wasn't what happened. Following the Communication Secretary's promise, the *News of the World* got its interview and pictures of Sophie, both conducted in the Belgian Suite at Buckingham Palace – quite a coup – to which it then added in bold three-inch print the arresting headline *MY EDWARD'S NOT GAY*.

The embarrassment and the mess didn't end there. Another tabloid had apparently been offered the story first but had turned it down, presumably not attaching any credibility to it. Feeling they had missed out on something newsworthy, editors became rather piqued.

Newspaper editors are apt to react robustly when nettled, and this one conformed to type, going into overdrive and running the Sophie sting story for a further week on both its front and inside pages. Meanwhile, the *News of the World*, no longer content with its exclusive interview, called the Palace the following Friday afternoon to report that because the tabloid in question had 'got it wrong' editors wanted the opportunity to 'set the record straight'. Which meant it was going to run the original story after all.

It became a big story. I could only look on from the wings and hope that everyone learned from it. But there was nothing we could do. The damage was done, and both Prince Edward and Sophie Wessex had to live with it.

My brief additional fortnight wasn't all about managing a firestorm of tabloid drama, however. Towards the end of my second week, there was room for some light relief.

One of Her Majesty's regular ceremonial commitments is the granting of audiences to overseas ambassadors. The average term for an ambassador based at his or her country's embassy in London is around three years, meaning that there is a pretty regular turnover.

To be accepted as an ambassador to the UK, the new incumbent has an audience with the Queen, at which he or she presents their credentials at a formal ceremony. In turn, the newly-appointed foreign ambassador or high commissioner presents his or her Letters of Credence or Letters of High Commission to Her Majesty. It is a regular commitment, so that particular week was just like any other, with an ambassador waiting in the Bow Room to be ushered into the 1855 Room for his audience with Her Majesty.

All ambassadors presenting credentials to the Queen also have a photograph taken with her. I was in the Marble Hall with a Press Association photographer waiting for the Queen to arrive and for us to be allowed in to the room ahead of the incoming ambassador.

As Her Majesty approached, her eyes landed on me. She did a double take while still on the move, somewhat surprised at seeing me.

She smiled. 'Dickie, what are you doing here?'

'Ah, well Your Majesty…I missed you so much, I just had to come back and see you.'

She didn't reply, but there was a definite twinkle in her eye.

What I had said in jest had been true in part. It had been good to catch up with former colleagues, and it was particularly good to bump into the Queen. Forget that she was the Sovereign, I had been blessed with astonishingly good fortune to have had such a great boss for a full dozen years.

But all good things must come to an end. A couple of days later I left the Palace for a second time, at the end of what turned out to be an unexpectedly eventful and rather amusing two-week tenure. I handed over my pass, said farewell and walked out of the Privy Purse door. It had been fun, but I felt no terrible pang of yearning. I had enjoyed 12 glorious years in what had turned out to be quite a showbizzy career choice, after all.

But now the show could go on without me.

CHAPTER 21

Retirement

September 2000

When I joined the Palace in 1988, I knew that come my birthday on 25th September, 2000, I would have to retire. While those of us employed by the Palace were not classed as Civil Servants, we did nevertheless fall under Civil Servant guidelines, which clearly mandated a retirement age of 60. Today, employees can continue on until they are 70, but sadly that was not the case in my day.

Once I reached my mid-50s, I began thinking about what I was going to do next, and fortunately it didn't take long for an answer to present itself. Over the course of my time at the Palace, I had learned and witnessed so much, gaining an insider's perspective of the inner workings of the Royal Family, which would lend significant credibility to my next venture.

My hope was that I would be able to return to the other side of the fence as a royal commentator. The beauty of commentary is that it is usually reliant upon common sense and fact, so I knew that I would not be breaking confidentiality in sharing my expertise.

I also thought lecturing on different aspects of the Monarchy was a possibility, as was leading media training courses and seminars. For many, retirement is met with a sense of finality and resignation. That was not the case with me.

After leaving the Palace on the eve of my 60th birthday, and allowing myself a day off on my actual birthday, I began a new job as a freelance royal commentator for the BBC the very next day.

The career switch also required an immediate personal transition. Leaving my position at Buckingham Palace meant that my wife and I had to move out of our apartment at Kensington Palace. We didn't move far, settling quickly and happily into a modest apartment south of Kensington High Street.

While professionally I was back in familiar territory, my new position did require a period of adjustment. Now freelance, I no longer had an office, nor did I have a community of work colleagues with whom to chew the fat as we drank our tea and coffee from bone china cups delivered to us by footmen. I was left to do my networking over countless breakfast and lunch meetings, and even the occasional dinner. It made for a busy schedule, and my working life continued to be, quite often, an around-the-clock affair.

It felt strange to have hopped the fence yet again, although strictly speaking, I was commentating now, rather than reporting.

There was a touch of irony in working for the BBC. I had tried to get my foot in the door there 26 years earlier, immediately following my return from Rhodesia. After they heard that my only prior experience had been with the Rhodesia Broadcasting Corporation, I was summarily shown the door. It was amazing to see the weight 12 years' experience at Buckingham Palace carried when it came time to seek new employment.

Working at the BBC offered a number of memorable experiences. Given my interest in ice-skating, the newsroom called me in to comment on Great Britain's chances for the 2002 Winter Olympics in Salt Lake City. I had already delivered one segment, and was in the green room waiting to do another when I noticed a sudden commotion. As people hurriedly shuffled in and out of the studio, the editor rushed towards me to say that Princess Margaret had died, and that I was to go back on-air immediately.

Due to the casual nature of the Olympics piece, I was dressed in a plain blue shirt and jeans. I hurried into the newsroom and borrowed a black jacket from one unsuspecting soul and a dark tie from another. I was on the air again within five minutes.

When the broadcast concluded I phoned my wife to have her run a suit down to the BBC studio. Since that day, I have always carried a suit in the back of my car with the appropriate ties.

My loud, colourful ties have become something of a talking point over the years. I have them specially hand painted by a lady named Jane Ireland, who has a stall in Covent Garden Market. Each one is unique, and I suppose they have become something of a trademark. I have often been asked if I wore them in front of the Queen. The answer is an unequivocal yes.

Did the Queen like them? Let me put it this way: Sometimes she would look at them as if to say *you can't be serious*. Other times, she would ignore them all together. Either way, no one ever told me *not* to wear them. Diana's opinion was expressed in action rather than words. She gave me a posh, albeit more conservative, Hermès tie for my birthday.

In addition to my continual work for the BBC, I also serve as a royal commentator for Sky News, ITV and Channel 5, as well as international news outlets in Canada, France, Germany, Italy, Poland, Russia, the Middle East, Japan, South Korea, Australia and New Zealand.

I am also a regular contributor to a number of high-profile cable and network news programs in the US, and have repeatedly worked with Larry King, Piers Morgan, Katie Couric and Elizabeth Vargas.

Once a royal commentator, always a royal commentator, I suppose, as my commitment to (and enthusiasm for) the work continues to this day.

Since finishing my time at the Palace, I have also had the privilege of doing a great deal of public speaking on all matters royal. This has not only provided me with regular work, but regular travel as well. My speaking agenda has led me to a wide and varied range of cities across the UK, USA, South Africa and beyond. Speaking on a number of cruise liners in particular has afforded me the opportunity to see places I might otherwise have never visited.

One of my most memorable cruises presented me with an extraordinary, if unexpected, two-day stop. The ship had originally been scheduled to port in Egypt, but due to political unrest at the time, the country was given a wide berth and it was decided that we would instead port in Haifa, Israel. We had ex-Royal Marines on board, as well as a Royal Navy liaison officer. A ship of that size normally cruises at 12 knots, but we sailed through pirate-infested waters at a speed of 20 knots. As darkness fell, all of the ship's deck lights were blacked out.

Israel was a country I had longed to visit. My mother had always rammed home to me, 'you were born a Jew, and you will die a Jew...what you do in between is your business.' As I had suddenly found myself with a couple of spare days in Haifa, I decided to join the ship's tour to Jerusalem.

The visit to the Western Wailing Wall was an awe-inspiring experience. I cannot describe how I felt facing the wall from just a few inches away. I had never practiced religion of any kind, and yet suddenly I felt completely at peace with the faith into which I had been born.

My second day in Haifa would prove equally emotional. Upon my mother and her brother Harry's arrival in the UK from Germany in 1939, Harry was quickly interned as a foreign alien and sent to Canada. Two years later, he was brought back to the UK and joined the airborne division of the Royal Army Service Corps. Having gone through the war unscathed, he was sent to British-mandated Palestine. I know nothing about his life from that point on, other than the fact that one day my mother received a telegram stating that Corporal Harry Stock had been murdered in hospital by an unknown assailant on Christmas Day. He was 24.

Harry was buried in the Commonwealth War Graves Cemetery in Haifa. My mother had visited his grave in the 1970s, and was saddened to find that his headstone bore the Christian Cross. She put in a request to the Commonwealth War Graves Commission to have it replaced with the Star of David.

That second day in Haifa, in early 2014, I visited Harry's headstone, which did indeed now bear the Star of David. I hadn't seen my uncle since 1947, and immediately found myself giving him an oral family history of the past 67 years. I spoke of my mother (his sister), of my daughter, Victoria, and of my grandson, Raff, before telling him a bit about myself. I think I did him proud, and came away completely drained.

I had been forced to give up skating at 17, when my mother and I moved to Rhodesia – a country decidedly lacking in ice rinks. I picked it up again at the age of 55, following a 38-year absence. I immediately rediscovered a passion for it. My skating life has literally come full circle, as once again I spend an inordinate amount of time at Queens... only this time around to the detriment of nothing.

Most days, when I'm not on a speaking tour or meeting television commitments, I can usually be found at the rink. Although I still enjoy skating as much as ever, it continues to get more difficult with age. As president of the dance club, my specialty is still dance. I do it as much as possible in spite of the fact that the ice time and music it requires has been severely curtailed over the years. I also teach group lessons for children of all ages, and have an organizational role in setting up class schedules for both students and my fellow instructors.

Another great pleasure I derive from Queens is producing the annual end-of-year charity show, which features a large number of our young students and adult staff members. One year we had 107 children participate in the show...and I'm pleased to report that not one of them fell over.

I will continue to skate for as long as I am fit and able to do so. It beats jogging or going to the gym. In 2005 I co-produced a semi-professional show to celebrate Queens's 75th anniversary. I vowed then and there that I would produce the show for its 100th anniversary. It is a vow I fully intend to keep, although I'll be aged 90 when the time comes.

The past 30 years of my life would not have been so thrilling had I not been able to share them with my wife, Rosemary.

After my divorce I did not actively seek marriage again, although I did experience times in which it would have been nice to have someone permanent in my life. After being a single father for seven years, I was also aware of the importance in Victoria's having a woman around to whom she could relate.

I was sitting in the LBC newsroom one day, passing the time between reading half-hour news bulletins, when my gaze fell onto a strewn copy of *Time Out*. While not my idea of a scintillating read, I began to thumb through it. Somehow I wound up in the 'lonely hearts' small ads. Put it up to fate, but my scanning eyes suddenly fell on the words: *Attractive blonde PR lady seeks...*

I must admit, something about the 'attractive blonde' part hooked me. With no more ado, I replied, enclosing one of my publicity pictures for good measure. I then thought nothing more of it.

Turns out the attractive blonde had recently come to the end of a relationship and placed the advertisement in *Time Out* at the instigation of friends during a merry dinner party. She, too, had then given it no more thought...at least until some weeks later when a bulky brown envelope arrived through her letter box, brimming with photographs of would-be suitors.

She had recognized my name, but initially put off responding because she was afraid I was doing a news story on lonely hearts. Fortunately, she changed her mind. Our initial drinks meeting went so well that I called her the next day to invite her to accompany Victoria and me to the ballet that weekend.

Silence.

It seems I had failed to mention the previous evening that I had a daughter.

She went on to accept the invitation.

Two days later, Rosemary called me regarding a professional matter. She had arranged a media event, but as so often happens, journalists who had confirmed invitations with her had cried off at the last minute. She needed me to help make up the numbers. The assignment did not exactly pertain to my royal beat, but I was more than happy to help the 'attractive blond PR lady' out of a jam.

It would be our third 'date' in less than a week, but I was already smitten. Taking the bull by the horns, I sent her flowers with a note that read: *Say it with flowers – William Penn, 1910. Will you marry me – Dickie Arbiter, 1984.*

Later that afternoon, as Rosemary busied herself arranging for roses to be sent to the journalists who had come through for her at the event (I wasn't the only one), her secretary called her and, somewhat timidly, informed her of the flowers I had sent...and of the note I had attached. Astounded, and more than a little panicked, Rosemary told her secretary to cancel the roses to me and send chrysanthemums instead.

I called Rosemary to thank her, and we arranged to meet again. Now face-to-face, I proposed once more. It would not be the last time.

My persistence eventually paid off. I met her in May 1984, and we married four months later. After an inevitable – and understandable – period of adjustment for both of them, Victoria and Rosemary forged a close relationship that still thrives to this day.

There is a school of thought that our honours system in the UK is unfair. For example, why is it that two sports stars of equal merit might be awarded honors at different levels? Why does one receive a Knighthood or Damehood while the other gets a CBE, OBE or MBE?

Honours come via the Government's Cabinet Office, and can be awarded at any time. In 1995 I was given an LVO (Lieutenant of the Royal Victorian Order). The Royal Victorian Order was founded in April 1896 by Queen Victoria as a way of rewarding personal service to the Sovereign. It is the one Order given solely at the discretion of the reigning Monarch, and does not have to pass through the government.

At the time, I was working with the Royal Collection, managing media relations for the Buckingham Palace summer opening and the restoration of Windsor Castle. I was delighted with the news that I would receive the Order, particularly when I learned that it would be listed in the Queen's Birthday Honours, published in June of that year.

It was given to me during a five-minute private audience with Her Majesty. At 12:55pm on Thursday, 18th July, as the Equerry announced me, I stood in the doorway to the 1855 Room, named for the Emperor Napoleon III and Empress Eugenie, who stayed in the room when they visited London that year.

I bowed my head before moving forward to be greeted the Queen. In her hand was a scarlet box with LVO stamped in gold on the front. She handed it to me with her left hand and shook my right as she said matter-of-factly, 'You've earned this.'

In response, I said only, 'Thank you, Your Majesty.'

We spoke briefly about the Palace summer opening and about the restoration at Windsor Castle before it was time for me to go.

Five minutes waiting for a bus feels like an age. Five minutes with the Queen flashes by in an instant.

With the exception of a second place trophy for go-cart racing with Diana in 1991 and certificates awarded by the Royal Drawing Society in 1954 and 1956, I have never won anything of substance.

In March 2014 my agent, Sylvia Tidy-Harris, called to say I had been invited to present an IRN/Sky News award to the most promising up-and-coming radio reporter. I accepted the invitation, and on the night presented the award at the appointed time before sitting down to watch the rest of the ceremony. As the evening drew to a close, IRN's former Managing Editor, John Perkins, took to the microphone and began to speak about a reporter who had made a name for himself in the days since joining LBC/IRN in 1974. As he continued it dawned on me that I was the reporter to whom he was referring. I glanced at Sylvia, who had been in on the ruse from the beginning. She looked back at me, the picture of innocence. The climax to John's tribute was the announcement of my first and only broadcasting award – The IRN/Sky News Gold Award, given for lifetime achievement in broadcasting.

I was flabbergasted. Though never short for words, I was rendered speechless. For all my bluster about awards, I really was tickled pink to have been recognized by my peers.

Penning this memoir has been something of a journey of discovery. Originally envisaged as a professional overview of an intense and turbulent time in the Royal Family's modern history, it soon developed into a memoir with a more personal flavour. Once I sat down and started thinking about my years of involvement with the Royal Family, it became impossible to leave my personal life, thoughts and feelings out of the material.

Prior to this writing, I don't think I had ever given much thought to the twists and turns that led me to my career path. Nor had I considered just how much of an influence strong, independent women had been in my life, a truism that continues to this day.

Take for example my mother. In reflecting on her abandonment of me in early childhood, I have found myself looking further back, to her own childhood in Germany, and to the abandonment by her mother. While there is no doubt that my mother was tough on me, I can see now that she was only teaching me how to be strong, even as she faced her own difficult challenges, of which there were many.

A young refugee when she arrived in the UK, not knowing a word of English, she soon found herself bringing a child into a war-torn world, though she was barely 19. It is difficult for one to accept her running away from my father at a time when he was so gravely ill, but one can only admire how hard she worked to make amends – doing her best to establish her independence, providing us with a good life in spite of the odds, even if doing so meant travelling half way round the world. No matter how many difficulties my peripatetic childhood presented, my mother never stopped expecting high standards from me. She worked tirelessly at her job until her retirement in her mid-60s, and was never prepared to accept second best.

I have spent much of my own personal life and career in the company of similarly tough, uncompromising and independent women. Perhaps my experience with my mother has helped me understand them better than I might have otherwise. I have worked and thrived with countless female broadcasters and journalists who have successfully staked their claim in a predominantly male world.

Then there is the young princess who had to mature from an intensely shy young debutante into a confident, level-headed public figure.

I can now see the parallels between Diana and my mother during her formative years. Both came from divorced backgrounds only to divorce at a young age themselves. Both learned to become reliant on a reserve of inner strength to get them through whatever life threw at them.

I have also begun to view my own personal trials against those of the royals around whom my career centered. As was the case with some of the royal marriages, the disintegration of my own first marriage was a source of great sadness. No child of divorce and separation wants the same for his or her children. I do not blame my ex-wife for anything. I had a job that often kept me away for long hours and long periods of time. Our union may well have been doomed from the start, as it is difficult to maintain a connection when so much time is spent apart.

That it was I who took on the lion's share of raising our daughter is perhaps surprising. But I felt I was well equipped to bring up Victoria alone precisely *because* of my own fractured childhood. I certainly wasn't daunted by the prospect of becoming a single parent. In my early life, it was all I ever knew.

No doubt I got some things wrong, but today I delight in the fact that my daughter has avoided many of my parental pitfalls in the raising of her own beautiful son. Victoria has developed many of her Grandmother's strengths, and to my joy has become an extremely capable and independent wife, mother and journalist.

The apple did not fall far from the tree. Still based in New York, Victoria is a respected writer and royal commentator for CNN. What a thrill it was to have her in London in the months leading up to Prince William's marriage to Catherine Middleton in 2011. There on assignment for CBS News, our paths crossed often during those harried months, and on the day of the royal wedding we even appeared on-air together for a segment for the Canadian network, CTV. It was a moment I will cherish always.

It is strange for me to think that in three successive generations of my family, the maternal figure left the home. My mother and her brother were left with their father in Aachen in 1932. My mother left me with my father at the age of four in 1944. My ex-wife, though still present in our daughter's life, left Victoria in my care at the age of three-and-a-half in 1977. They say things run in threes. I certainly hope our pattern stops there.

Of all the strong women who have influenced me, there are none quite like my boss of 12 years – Her Majesty the Queen. My memory of washing up with her (or drying up, as was the case) is just as delightful to recall today as it was when it actually happened.

By any measure Her Majesty is a remarkable woman. Faithfully supported by her husband, the Duke of Edinburgh, for more than 66 years, she is the first to admit that she could not carry out her role without his loyalty and love. It is true that by anyone's standards she lives a life of privilege and comfort – a primary source of contention for many of her detractors.

What cannot be argued, however, is Her Majesty's sheer commitment to duties that she wasn't even been born to do. Though well beyond retirement age, she maintains a seven-day working week, performing a job for which she has racked up more than six decades of experience, and one for which – unlike some of her European counterparts – she personally receives no pay.

She is also capable of the most exceptional acts of kindness. The Windsor Castle restoration was completed (under budget and ahead of schedule) on the fifth anniversary of the fire, also the day of her 50th wedding anniversary. The anniversary ball, to which I was invited, was to be the first function held in the newly restored castle. However, I felt that it would be appropriate to first host a thank-you reception for the workers who had so admirably completed the restoration.

The idea was accepted, and on Friday, 14th November, 1997, Her Majesty and the Duke of Edinburgh hosted a reception for 1500 members of the workforce in order to thank them personally for their service. This was no jolly for CEOs and executives, rather an evening in honour of the men and women who had rolled up their sleeves and literally delivered the nuts and bolts of such an ambitious undertaking.

At a reception of this kind, Her Majesty and the Duke of Edinburgh would normally stay no more than 90 minutes. So pleased was the Queen with the finished work, however, that they stayed for two hours, a gesture that did not go unnoticed by those being honoured.

Our Queen is also reliable to a fault. She never gives less than a 100 percent, and never fails to fully engage with those fortunate enough to meet her. But she also has a deep awareness of the needs of her family, which is rarely witnessed by members of the public. I experienced this for

ON DUTY WITH THE QUEEN

myself when I spent a day at Windsor before an upcoming State Visit.

At lunch I was seated next to an ailing Princess Margaret who, following various bouts of ill health, had suffered an unfortunate scalding accident that had left her in a wheelchair. She was a shadow of her former garrulous self. The Princess wore wraparound sunglasses throughout the meal and was doggedly monosyllabic, deflecting every polite conversational opener I tried to send her way.

I felt sorry for her. While I'm sure it was good for her to be among company, I'm not sure the Princess felt quite up to it. Ever observant, the Queen seemed to have drawn the same conclusion. Later at dinner, I was seated next to Her Majesty and she brought up the subject almost immediately; we exchanged a few words and sympathetic smiles, and the conversation moved on. Needless to say she always seemed to have a strong yet subtle connection with every member of her family.

Having feared at 55 that retirement would prove to be something of a challenge to one as active and driven as myself, I am pleased to report at 74 that my years since leaving the Palace have been some of the most fulfilling of my life. While it is gratifying to reflect on my unique and varied career, I also eagerly anticipate the years ahead, which will no doubt include an opportunity to commentate on the Queen's Platinum Jubilee in 2022.

Epilogue

Summer 2014

Her Majesty Queen Elizabeth II is Britain's 40th monarch, and only the sixth queen to have ruled since William the Conqueror took the crown of England over a thousand years ago. Though she may be taken for granted in some quarters, she has notched up many impressive statistics over the course of her 62-year reign.

Representing the country's interests abroad, the Queen has travelled to 116 countries and undertaken 261 official overseas tours, including 96 State Visits (in which one head of state invites another to visit his or her country). It is quite difficult to gauge a precise tally, but by conservative estimates, she has undertaken more than 30,000 engagements in the United Kingdom alone, and in doing so has met people from all walks of life. She has welcomed over a million and a half people to garden parties at Buckingham Palace and the Palace of Holyrood House. She has conferred over 410,000 honours at more than 650 investitures, and as the United Kingdom's second longest reigning monarch, she shows only marginal signs of slowing down, and none of giving up. Queen Victoria reigned for 63 years and 216 days. God willing, Her Majesty will break that record on 9th September, 2015.

It is inevitable, however, that the Queen's reign will end, and that her place will be inherited by her son, the Prince of Wales. This is the nature of the Monarchy. The cast is ever changing, and there are many royalists who follow those changes avidly. Despite the protestations of cynics and anti-monarchists, the Royal Family's popularity is far from waning.

At the time of Diana's death, newspaper reports suggested that there would never be another royal funeral as widely spectated. The assumption was that when the Queen Mother passed away, public sentiment would be fairly indifferent. While it would be met with great sadness, her death at a grand old age would not be as shocking as Diana's untimely demise. When the Queen Mother did pass away in her sleep at the age of 101 in 2002, it was clear that the press had got it wrong.

A vast majority of the British population had grown up with Queen Elizabeth The Queen Mother. An estimated 200,000 mourners paid their respects to her as she lay in state in Westminster Hall. On the day of her funeral hundreds of thousands more lined the route from the service in Westminster Abbey to the interment in St George's Chapel, Windsor.

Similarly, later in 2002, when Buckingham Palace announced plans for the Golden Jubilee weekend (marking the Queen's 50 years on the throne), the usual newspaper doom-and-gloom merchants suggested that no-one was interested and that the whole thing would flop like a damp squib.

Wrong again. It was in fact cause for national celebration. Between February and August of that year, the Queen and the Duke of Edinburgh visited 70 cities and towns across England, Scotland, Wales and Northern Ireland, as well as 50 counties.

Her Majesty travelled more than 40,000 miles around the world to countries including Jamaica, New Zealand, Australia and Canada.

A special website launched for the Golden Jubilee received over 28 million hits during a six-month period. Over 3,000 members of the media from more than 60 countries were accredited to cover the central Jubilee weekend in London at the beginning of June.

Throughout the weekend, one million-plus people gathered daily outside Buckingham Palace and all the way down the Mall to Trafalgar Square to celebrate the Queen's distinguished reign. Hardly the 'damp squib' the press had predicted at the beginning of the year.

When the 2012 Diamond Jubilee came around a decade later, no-one was surprised that it, too, was a resounding success. Despite the miserable weather over the course of that celebratory four-day weekend, more than a million people gathered every day at Buckingham Palace and at events throughout London. Crowd levels mirrored those of 2002, again trailing all the way down the Mall to Trafalgar Square.

Whatever the media says, a large percentage of the

British population loves its Royal Family, and the institution of monarchy continues to endure, always evolving, just as it has done for the last 1,000 years. It is by any standard a robust and resilient establishment.

That's not to say there haven't been some blips in terms of the line of succession. Charles I had his head disconnected from his shoulders in 1649, and tragically, despite 17 pregnancies, Queen Anne died leaving no surviving children in 1707, thus ending the reign of the House of Stuart. But due to the Act of Settlement that same year, what followed was a memorable and largely harmonious period with the newly-established House of Hanover having come to eminence. Georges I, II and III followed, but as a result of George IV's daughter having predeceased him, he was left with no natural successor upon his death in 1830.

The crown passed to his brother, the Duke of Clarence, who became William IV. Although he had ten illegitimate children with Dora Jordan, a very well-known Irish actress in her day, not one of his five legitimate children with Queen Adelaide survived him. Upon his death he was succeeded by his dead brother's daughter, Victoria, who became Queen in 1837. Victoria's marriage to Prince Albert saw the end of the House of Hanover. The royal house of Saxe-Coburg and Gotha was established in 1842.

There was another near-catastrophic blip at the end of 1936 when Edward VIII abdicated and his reluctant brother, Albert, or, as he was affectionately known, Bertie, acceded, becoming George VI. It was that momentous event and subsequent change of direction that led to the young Princess Elizabeth succeeding to the British throne in 1952.

The new generation of senior royals are now hard at work establishing their own roles within 'The Firm' – a moniker coined by Prince Philip. Prince William, having completed his three years as a search and rescue helicopter pilot at RAF Valley in Anglesey, Wales, is playing a more active role, carving out a niche for himself, as well as supporting his grandmother, the Queen. William is also a fiercely private young man aiming to achieve for his own family something he never had growing up – a stable environment for his baby son, Prince George.

Harry has served two tours of operational duty in Afghanistan, one in 2008 and the second in 2013. As has now been widely reported, the first of Harry's tours was, with the co-operation of the media, kept a tightly guarded secret.

The thinking at the time was that if his presence was publicised, he and his fellow comrades would become a prime target for the enemy. This became an all too real concern when German newspaper *Bild* and Australian magazine *New Idea* broke the embargo and documented the Prince's deployment. In response to this major breach, the UK's Ministry of Defense decided to err on the side of caution and withdrew Harry after only ten weeks of his planned three-month deployment.

On reflection it was probably the right thing to do. A government doesn't spend tens of thousands of pounds training a soldier only to have him sit at home twiddling his thumbs.

It was perhaps inevitable that Harry's second tour as an Apache helicopter pilot with the Army Air Corps *was* well publicised, and thankfully he completed his tour without incident.

As of this writing Prince Harry has returned to the Household Cavalry Regiment, where he has undertaken a desk job at HQ London District on Horse Guards. His current role involves helping to co-ordinate significant projects and commemorative events that involve the army in London, while at the same time (his military duties permitting), carrying out more official engagements on behalf of the family. Stories regarding Harry's on-again/off-again romances continue to dominate newspaper columns, but for now his one true passion continues to be his involvement with the Invictus Games, hosted in London in September 2014.

While William is generally regarded as the more measured and serious of the two brothers, Harry has been tagged by the media as a bit of a wild child. In his early 20s he was the epitome of royal paparazzi fodder, often making front page news for all the wrong reasons – leaving night clubs a little worse for wear, being photographed wearing a WWII German Afrika Korps uniform with a swastika arm band and getting caught drinking under-age and smoking cannabis.

On the whole the British press does treat the Princes pretty fairly. Occasionally Harry is taken to task for his errors in judgment – accepting a skiing holiday to Kazakhstan, for example. Given the country's less-than-stellar human rights record, and considering there were any number of ski resorts he could have visited, his advisors should have given Kazakhstan the thumbs down. Likewise, it wasn't a particularly brilliant decision for Prince William to go hunting in Spain in February 2014, the day before he was due to launch a high-profile campaign to end the illegal wildlife trade.

Unfortunately, there is still a belief within the Royal

Family that the details surrounding private visits or holidays are on a purely need-to-know basis. In other words, to them private is private and their advisors don't need to know.

Prince Harry is quick learner, however, and he doesn't make the same mistake twice. Another of his attributes is his ability to muck in as part of a team. In 2013 he joined the Walking With the Wounded South Pole Allied Challenge, for which he joined 12 injured servicemen and women from the UK, USA and the Commonwealth. He took on the expedition in his own right, as a serviceman rather than as a royal. The teams trekked 200 miles in appalling conditions before finally reaching the South Pole on December 13th – proof that with the right team and the right attitude, anything is possible.

This particular generation of royals rising through the ranks is made up of doers. No longer are royals merely showing up to cut ribbons, unveil plaques or plant trees. Today they are getting stuck in at ground level. In December 2009 Prince William spent a night sleeping rough on the streets of London in an effort to highlight the work of the homeless charity Centrepoint of which he is patron. In March 2011 Prince Harry joined a team of injured servicemen for the first five days of their trek to the North Pole, and in early 2014 the Princes showed up announced in Datchet, Berkshire to help the local community with flood relief. This commitment to others is something for which Diana would have been especially proud. That the Princess left this world too soon goes without saying, but she was with her sons just long enough to ingrain in them a deep seeded understanding of those less fortunate.

One area in which the Princes continue to struggle is in

their relationship with the media. They know they need the press in the same way the press needs them, but they wrestle with what truly is private, and what is worthy of public interest. Diana did court the attention of the media from time to time, but the flip side of that coin was that she often complained of feeling hunted and haunted. William and Harry saw it all, and they are savvy enough to avoid falling into the same trap. For now they are striking a good balance, working to their own agenda rather than one set by the media, but it is a delicate balance that can shift at any time.

2014 has seen the Queen's popularity riding higher than it ever has in her 62 years on the throne. The British monarchy has survived executions, divorces, illicit affairs, illegitimate children and wildly eccentric behaviour on the part of its kings and queens, but it continues to persevere. Republicanism, with a popularity rating in the region of 13 percent, has been around for centuries, but the anti-monarchist group Republic declared in 2012 that, 'The Queen is untouchable.'

In spite of her many public triumphs she has endured many personal sorrows. Having been brought up to believe that divorce was un-royal, during her own tenure the Queen has had to deal with the divorce of her sister, Princess Margaret, as well as the subsequent divorces of three of her four children. In 1979 Lord Louis Mountbatten, beloved uncle of Prince Philip, was assassinated by IRA terrorists while out on his fishing boat in County Sligo, Ireland. In 2002, the Queen also suffered the loss of her own much-loved mother and sister within a seven week period. All of this occurred under the watchful gaze of the media. I don't believe any elected head of state would survive or even tolerate the constant media scrutiny, invasion of privacy and irrational prejudice that the Queen has had to abide decade after decade. With no alternative but to carry on, she has done so unflinchingly.

From time to time the ugly word 'abdication' creeps in, never more so than when Queen Beatrix of Holland abdicated in January 2013. At 75 she thought it was time for the younger generation to take over. King Albert II of the Belgians, aged 78, followed suit shortly after, stepping down in July 2013 after a string of scandals and controversies. Most recently, 76-year-old King Juan Carlos of Spain stepped down citing ill health in June 2014. Will the Queen, an octogenarian, follow suit? In a word, no.

She was never destined to become Queen, but she has dedicated her life to service and duty. During a radio address on the occasion of her 21st birthday, Princess Elizabeth said – 'I declare before you all that my whole life whether it be long or short shall be devoted to your service and the service of our great imperial family to which we all belong' – a declaration she reaffirmed at her Silver (1977), Golden (2002) and Diamond (2012) Jubilees.

The Queen's public image has noticeably softened in recent years, as made apparent during her visit to Northern Ireland in June 2014. It was an open visit, meaning it was announced, and not shrouded in secrecy due to security concerns, as had been the norm in the past. This time much of her itinerary was made public, which gave the Queen the opportunity to engage with the people of Belfast.

The headlines said it all:

Queen ushers in new normal!

The Queen, up close and personal thrills the crowds!

The Queen makes astonishing jail visit with former IRA commander, Martin McGuinness!

Her Majesty would be the first to accept that no matter how painful, life moves on. By building bridges in Northern Ireland, the Queen is ensuring that she leaves a monarchy in good stead with friendships reaffirmed and hands of forgiveness shaken. The world is changing rapidly and, like their grandmother, Princes William and Harry must continue to adapt and evolve to meet the needs of the 21st century. During the Diamond Jubilee's Buckingham Palace balcony appearance, the Queen sent out a very clear message regarding the future of the Monarchy. Instead of the entire family stepping out as is custom following the Trooping of the Colour ceremony, she was joined only by her heir, the Prince of Wales, his heir, the Duke of Cambridge (along with their wives) and Prince Harry, who was third in line at the time.

With the 2013 arrival of its newest member, HRH Prince George of Cambridge, the Royal Family can take comfort in knowing that the Crown is secure for generations to come. Though still only a baby, George stands to be the first British Monarch of the 22nd century.

As for me, I very much doubt I will be around to see George crowned King George VII, but what I do know with certainty is that the day it happens, the whole world will be watching.

Dickie Arbiter, June 2014

Glossary

Belgian Suite, The: Named after Leopold I, uncle of Prince Albert and first king of the Belgians, this suite of rooms is used by all State Visitors, guests of the Queen, and is where the Obamas slept during their visit in 2011

Bow Room: The Bow Room is familiar to the many thousands of guests to Royal Garden Parties who pass through it on their way to the garden

BP: Buckingham Palace

BST: British Summer Time

Chinese Dining Room, the: Originally called the Chinese Luncheon Room during the reign of Queen Victoria its furnishings come from George IV's 19th Century folly – the Brighton Pavillion

Civil List: Royal income – money given by the state to support the Queen, indirectly from the taxpayers. This has now changed to the Sovereign's Grant, which comes direct from the Crown Estates

DCMS: Government Department of Culture, Media and Sport

Equerry: Military officer on personal attendance to the Queen or senior male member of the Royal Family

FCO: the Foreign and Commonwealth Office; a government ministry responsible for foreign affairs – similar to the state department in the USA

Folly: An elaborate and eccentric building that's of absolutely no use to anyone

HM: Her Majesty

KP: Kensington Palace

Narwhal: A small Arctic whale, the male of which has a long forward-pointing spirally twisted tusk developed from one of its teeth

PPO: Personal Protection Officer – armed Scotland Yard police officer

Privy Purse: The finance section responsible for the financial management of the public funding granted to the Royal Household in the form of the Sovereign Grant

Scruff Order: Casual dress code, usually trousers and open necked shirt, no tie or jacket required – jeans acceptable occasionally

Spare: When Harry was born he was called a spare to his brother, in other words a third in line to the throne. Now he is fourth in line, and when and if the Duke and Duchess of Cambridge have more children, Harry will move further down the line of succession

Suite car: A car used to carry members of the household in attendance on the principal/s – press secretary, equerry and lady in waiting, if the latter two were not individually travelling with the principal

SUV: Sports utility vehicle (or 4x4)

TRH: Their Royal Highnesses

Yachtie: Royal Yacht seaman

1844 Room: So named after its occupation by Emperor Nicholas of Russia in 1844 as a guest of Queen Victoria

1855 Room: So named after Emperor Napoleon III and Empress Eugenie who stayed in the room when they visited Queen Victoria

Index